The Androcles effect

Androcles faced the most terrifying of man-eating lions ever to enter an ancient Roman Colosseum. But the gentle fellow had a way of taming the ferocious beast. He simply whispered into its ear and it abandoned all thought of eating him. Summoned to the royal box, Androcles was asked his secret by the emperor.

'It's this, my lord. I merely tell the lion that, as soon as he's finished dinner, he'll be asked to just say a few words.'

If Androcles has whispered in your ear, my friend, let the next few pages help to restore your lion's courage.

BOB MONKHOUSE'S

Complete Speaker's Handbook

**Illustrations by
Ian Dicks**

Published in Great Britain in 2004 by
Virgin Books
Thames Wharf Studios
Rainville Road
London W6 9HA

First published 1988 as *Just Say A Few Words* by Lennard Publishing

ISBN 0 7535 09083

A catalogue record for this book is available from the British Libary

Editor Michael Leitch
Design by Paul Cooper
Typesetting by Phoenix Photosetting, Chatham, Kent
Printed and bound in Great Britain by Mackays of Chatham, Chatham, Kent

Contents

Introduction

When Bob Monkhouse died in December 2003, his fellow entertainer Des O'Connor said it was as if 'one of the brightest lights on the Christmas tree just went out'. He also went on to say that whenever Bob arrived at a function or cabaret he would always have prepared material that was specially written for the occasion, such was his professionalism.

In *The Complete Speaker's Handbook*, which was originally published as *Just Say A Few Words*, Bob Monkhouse shares with the reader the knowledge that he accumulated about speaking in public.

As only he could, Bob said in his original introduction that if you are one of those people who have said that they're more frightened of making a speech than they are of disease, bankruptcy or a mother-in-law's visit, then he could help you. He continued: 'With this book as your guide you can learn the simple steps that will help you become a confident and effective speaker. Read it and you will find out how to overcome nervousness and make you tension work for you. Follow my techniques and you will find that few means of communication are as rewarding as public speaking. And the learning process is fun.

'Michael Parkinson once told me that hosting a chat show is the oldest activity in television. He described it as 'two consenting adults performing an unnatural act in public'. Well, making a speech isn't a natural activity. It's a performance, a show, a piece of artifice that needs the right sort of preparation, polish and practice. There's no lazy way – but I can show you short cuts and tricks of the trade that you'll enjoy using.

'This is not a book for veteran professional speakers, although even those interpid warhorses will find many new insights and tips. There's also a fund of fresh one-liners and modernised classics of humour never published before. What's more, I've tested the worth of every one of them in many a banqueting hall and ballroom before recommending them here, so you don't have to wade through a lot of duds.

'I've written this guide for those people who are required, just occasionally, to rise before a wedding party, a club meeting, a business gathering, or any cluster of unnervingly attentive faces to just say a few words. I've kept it simple and chatty because that is the language of easy communication. And easy communication is what speech-given is all about.

'We'll begin with the basic stuff, ways to focus your thoughts and gather ideas. Then we'll explore ways of constructing a speech, assessing the audience's needs, and projecting your most effective image from entrance to exit.

'Special sections examine the deadpan delivery of humour, how to let your ideas grow, and the best uses of triviality to emphasis your most serious messages. How to begin a speech is a subject which deserves several interesting approaches and gets them, likewise the ways in which you can construct the middle and end of what you want to say.

'I'll demonstrate every method I know of creating an amusing and informative speech. I'll explain the secrets of performance techniques, how to stimulate spontaneity, plus your impact on the audience, and how to command their attention. Together we can establish a set of ground rules in your mind that will enable you to deal with any situation that calls upon you to speak to a group of humans, whether they're your family, sales force, voters, a bunch of kids, a debating society, shop-floor workers, boardroom directors, monks, drunks, punks, academicians, statisticians, rag-trade philosophers, newspaper cynics, pundits, bandits, cops, fops, chums, bums or twenty-six million viewers. But in exchange for whatever I can give you, you have to promise me something.

'Give me your time and your mind. Join me wholeheartedly in this endeavour and it will pay greater dividends than you can imagine. You'll be surprised how much pleasure and fulfilment are to be had from speaking well in public. And applause is a terrific reward. Just ask the person who gets it.

'Keep this book somewhere you can easily find it. Stow it in the loo if you like. But please, don't use its pages for any purpose other than reference!'

First steps

If, say, you are a businessman used to corporate terms you may feel the language of entertainment is unsuitable for your kind of public speaking. You employ financial, industrial and commercial idioms, and that is the language you are comfortable with.

True, but in the very moment you rise to talk to an audience, you also step onto the stage. When you open your mouth to speak, you enter show business. The more you can accept that, the more successful you will be.

Today people have become pretty sophisticated about what entertains them and what does not. The old magic and mystery of the theatre no longer create wonder along with amusement. The public knows how the tricks are done and its patience with an unsatisfactory performance has grown short. Sometimes I've suspected entire theatre audiences of holding imaginary remote controls with their thumbs on the off-button. Merely to gain and hold their attention requires showmanship. But this is something that can be acquired.

MAKE IT SOUND GOOD

I am sure you know of some executive who is sought after as a speaker because he has learned to make himself impressive. His audience may know next to nothing about his firm, the British Stuff Manufacturing Co. Ltd, but when this chap starts talking, they listen. He's confident, he's informative, and everyone can understand each point he makes. He keeps them interested in what he's going to say next and, every now and then, he scores a comfortable laugh. When he sits down, that audience will regard the British Stuff Manufacturing Co. Ltd differently. The firm and what it does will have become a familiar and friendly part of life.

This is fact, not fancy. Every accomplished communicator in the world of business knows it to be true. And doesn't it make sense?

If we face an important interview, we prepare ourselves to make the best possible impression. We look good. So, if we are about to meet an audience, we should polish our words as well as our shoes. We should sound good. Let's make that a first resolution.

BE YOUR OWN WRITER

Let's assume that you are prepared to do all your own background work – researching and writing the lines for the performance that you will eventually deliver. There are, of course, companies that offer script-writing services for a fee, and there is nothing to stop you from going to them if you wish. I have assumed, however, that you would not be reading this book if you were content to lean on a professional speechwriter. So, that makes two fields you need to conquer – the preparation of the speech, followed by its delivery. Where, though, do you begin? How do you go about getting your act together?

All speeches consist of a cleverly joined string of solutions to the cry 'But I haven't an idea what to say.' Ideas are the core and foundation of the whole thing, and collecting ideas is your starting point.

Try and keep a notebook handy and, from this moment on, please use it to jot down anything you read or hear that just might be useful in a speech, no matter how remote the possibility. You might hear some wag in a pub say, 'Did you know the war between Iran and Iraq was caused by a typing error?' and get a laugh for it. Just as soon as you can, note down 'IRAN IRAQ TYPING ERROR'. Maybe you'll never use it. But it might fit neatly into an address to your company about the purchase of new and expensive computers: 'Better machinery can lead to fewer mistakes. And a single slip can cost more than an entire system. Good heavens, just look at the war between Iran and Iraq – all caused by a typing error.'

Ideas are Like Beanshoots – They Grow in the Dark

Originality wells up from mysterious and subconscious sources, said Charles Horton Cooley, the American thinker, and you must let the subterranean waters accumulate. Haven't you found that you can go to bed totally stumped for a solution to some problem, and wake up the next morning with an inspired answer? The same trick can come to your aid in preparing a speech.

Putting the matter to the back of your mind triggers that marvellous part of the brain where subconsciousness dwells. By concentrating your thoughts on the possible ways in which you could express your message you are also awakening your own instinctive ability to recognise the best method. And not only in sleep. Most professional writers know that the creative process can take place during all those times of the day when they are occupied with prosaic matters – shaving, taking a bath, mowing the lawn, walking the dog, even going to the loo.

Especially going to the loo, according to Noel Coward. He found that daily function was frequently accompanied by the arrival of a pleasing inspiration. Kingsley Amis too, wrote of his reliance upon casual meditation while carrying out some undemanding task or other, finding the rewards were his when he reached the typewriter and began to write. So much has already fallen into place. You are not faced with a dreaded sheet of blank paper but with a welcome page on which to arrange the ideas which have been floating to the surface of your mind and which now seem to demand expression.

So don't put off contemplating until the last minute. Muse as you munch, weigh while you wash, ponder when you perambulate; every pensive reflection will pay dividends when the time comes to collect your thoughts and say them out loud to an audience.

Your script – putting the right construction on it

It's time to lay out the shape of your speech and look at the basic elements in its construction. Lewis Carroll's White Rabbit was given some pretty clear advice:

'Where shall I begin, please your Majesty?' he asked.

'Begin at the beginning,' the King said, gravely, 'and go on till you come to the end: then stop.'

IN THE BEGINNING

In the beginning is the hook. In show business terms a hook is any means of grabbing the crowd. Any good salesman uses various opening gambits to engage the attention of his customers. They range from the market trader's

'Son, have I got a deal for you!' to the softer sell of 'Don't rush me, these are like gold dust.' One smooth talker opened his pitch to me with 'I'm selling these computers below cost.' I said, 'How can you make money like that?' He said, 'Repairing them.' I laughed so much, I nearly bought one.

The start of every public presentation has a hook to it. Think of stage plays. In *The Man of Destiny* George Bernard Shaw shows us the 27-year-old Napoleon Bonaparte attacking all the courses of his meal simultaneously with his left hand while marking military positions on a map. He calls for some red ink. The landlord of the Italian inn says, 'Alas! Excellency, there is none.' Napoleon answers, 'Then kill something and bring me its blood.' The grinning host replies that there is nothing but the general's own horse, the sentinel, the lady upstairs and his wife. Napoleon says, 'Kill your wife.' 'Willingly, your Excellency,' replies the man, 'but unhappily I am not strong enough. She would kill me.' 'That will do equally well,' says Napoleon. During this wonderful exchange, we're wondering about the lady upstairs. We're hooked.

A great playwright such as Shaw knows that he has us at his disposal for the duration of Act One at least, so he has no need to grab us by the lapels from curtain-up, merely to put us in an interested state of mind. But remember that, as he planned his plays, shaped his plots and deployed his characters, he had a tough decision to make – where to start. No drama or novel ever has a single obvious starting point, there are hundreds to choose from. Who speaks first? How far into the story are we? How early was the outcome determined?

We have a similar choice to make with our speech. Should we go in loud and wake 'em up? Creep quietly and lure them into listening? Use the carrot or the stick? The manner of your approach depends greatly upon your personal style and the image of yourself that you wish to project. But there are useful professional devices for taking charge of your audience and here are three – the Question, the Anniversary and the Surprise.

The Question Hook

Start by asking a question. It's a common enough oratorical ruse but often forgotten by speakers in the mildly nervous grip of composing that opening paragraph. The Question Hook can take many forms but we'll look at four dependable examples. First, the question that's immediately relevant to the people, the place and the time.

Question One: Special for Tonight

An expert on nutrition kicked off his after-dinner address by waving the menu in the air and asking, 'How many calories do you think you've just consumed? How much protein? How much fat? How much carbohydrate? How much cholesterol or alcohol? Well, I am about to tell you and the answers will not only amaze you and amuse you, they will make you very proud of what your body can do.'

This approach engaged everyone's attention because it was topical, personal and, although a little worrying, it contained a promise of good news. A similar strategy might suit you. Maybe there's something unique about the occasion: 'What is it about this evening that makes it different from any other?' Or perhaps the audience has achieved a goal which you are about to announce: 'Let me ask you a question about yourselves. Why have you, each and every one of you, a reason to feel proud today?'

That last application of the Question Hook introduces the second example.

Question Two: Let's Think About Ourselves

You open with a question that makes everyone present ask it of themselves. 'If you had to describe yourself as a saint or a sinner, which would it be? No, seriously, do you think you're an angel or a devil? Put it this way: are you more good than bad or more bad than good? Now be careful. If any of you claim to be 100 per cent saintly, just remember this – a halo is only 10 inches from being a noose.'

That speech went on to praise the charitable work of the audience while listing their daily sins with accuracy and good humour. The question had caused everyone in the room to make a small private assessment of themselves and made them readier to pay attention to what followed. This prodding of a person's ego may seem more like a conversational trick at a party, but it really does suit some speeches very well indeed.

I heard a Queen's Counsel begin, 'Think carefully before you answer this question, and I address it to each one of you individually. Have you ever broken the law?' It made a neat start to a list of small infringements that most of us commit regularly and unknowingly. Such questions help to involve the audience in subject matter that might not otherwise seem so attractive at first. If the body of your speech is a bit heavy, consider introducing it lightly with that sort of question.

Question Three: Off the Wall

Next there's the question that appears to have no relevance whatsoever. A social reformer began, 'Why are there so many questions to which no-one knows the answers? Anybody?' He looked around so earnestly his audience couldn't help laughing at the intrinsic absurdity of what he was asking. Then he went on, 'No, I don't know either. But I've got quite a few answers to questions not enough of us bother to ask. And in offering you these answers I may step on a few toes today. Well, if I do I shall have to take comfort in the words of Winston Churchill: "Any man who never steps on anyone else's toes is standing still!"'

By the way, it's worth noting that Churchill never said that. I've always found that attributing a good line to an admired wit increases its appreciation. Again, if I've got an old quip that's funny but familiar, I'll attribute it to a respected but dead comedian. Nobody argues about it, I'm not responsible for sounding corny and, as the audience laughs at the gag, I can see some of them nodding in apparent recollection of having heard it from the great late comic. I've even known a totally new pun that would normally pull a groan of agony from the crowd become magically transformed through wholly false attribution to Disraeli or Groucho Marx and score both hoots of mirth and nostalgic applause. 'So what's to hurt?' as Lord Louis Mountbatten was always saying.

Question Four: Making Them Wonder

Lastly, a fourth version of the Question Hook is the presentation of a small mystery to the audience. In this example it was applied to a fairly serious and successful business gathering.

'There is a quality present in this room, a certain positive charge that I can sense very clearly. Every public speaker develops an instinctive feeling for unusual vibrations and this evening there is one powerful unifying force that I find quite unmistakable. What is it?' The pause need not be a long one before presenting the answer: 'In a word – confidence. Behind us lies a great year for our industry, before lies an even greater one. And you are the reason, you are the do-ers. While others have hesitated, you have acted. You've seen the size of the job and you've tackled it. You've learned the wisdom of what my old granddad used to say: "You can't plough a field by turning it over in your mind."'

Having flattered his audience quite enough, the speaker is now free to emphasise the very weaknesses in the industry that he may have been setting out to identify in the first place. Because he has praised the audience, they will be more willing to receive his criticisms.

There are countless ways to employ the Question Hook. It can also come in handy as a way of closing: 'And let me leave you with this question .... '

The Anniversary Hook

'Ladies and gentlemen, this is an historic day! This day, the 17th of December, will always be memorable for three great events. Orville Wright made the first successful flight in a petrol-driven plane in 1903, Ludwig Van Beethoven had his first day on earth in 1770 – and on this day in 2001 you attended tonight's banquet and heard the finest damned after-dinner speech of your entire lifetime! Now ... who's going to make it?'

There's nothing like telling the people what a special day it is today. It has a feeling of topicality, even if the anniversaries named are ancient history, because you are telling them that 'Today's the Day!' But where do you find such handy facts? There are quite a few reference books in the public libraries listing the chronology of great discoveries, births and deaths, publications, wars and battles, performances, treaties, exhibitions, laws, Nobel awards, inventions, statistics, sports events, films, plays, paintings, economic and political events, even momentous speeches. Alas, few of them are very entertaining.

Back in 1981 I wrote one myself called *The Book of Days*, 365 pages of noteworthy events plus light-hearted comments. While I expected it to come in handy for disc jockeys, I've been surprised at the number of public speakers who have told me of its usefulness to them. One wrote, 'Whenever I'm stuck for an odd coincidence or a legitimate chuckle to get me off the ground I just check the date of the speech in the book and find some historical curiosity. One Leap Year I was desperate for a line to open a talk to a Musical Society on the last day of February – and there it was.'

The item he found under 29 February ran: 'Gioacchino Antonio Rossini was born today in 1792 in Pesaro, Italy. He wrote thirty-nine operas, including *The Barber of Seville* in 1816 and *William Tell* in 1829. When his 1826 opera *The Siege of Corinth* received a derogatory review, Rossini wrote to the critic: "Sir, I am sitting in the smallest room of my house. I have your review before me. In a moment it will be behind me."'

Anniversaries, births and deaths are always worth checking up on and you can usually find a selection in *The Times*, *Daily Telegraph* and some Sunday papers. Not only can they provide natural openers, you'll find them equally useful for wrapping up a speech as well. For instance, September the 6th.

'In conclusion, ladies and gentlemen, this day marks another significant anniversary. On this day, September the 6th, back in 1901, US President William McKinley was making a speech when some fellow shot him dead. Now I'm not much of a one for believing in signs and omens but there's no point in tempting fate so I think I'll sit down.'

The Surprise Hook

'Before I start speaking, I have something to say,' said one speaker and was bewildered by the laughter it provoked. He'd been delivering the same packaged twenty minutes for years but had just been asked to put in a preliminary announcement. What was so damned funny about that?

This speaker's unintentional absurdity points to another of the trade's opening stratagems – the unexpected statement or the Surprise Hook. By putting a startling remark ahead of your formal discourse, you catch the audience off-guard.

For example, it can be the expression of an attitude directly opposed to that commonly held, a small heresy that will create a shock-wave of attention. Imagine rising to address an enthusiastic Angling Society with these words:

'Fishing is the closest you can come to doing nothing at all without getting into politics.'

After the briefest pause to let that unorthodox view register, you might add:

'Of course, I'm talking about *my* fishing, not yours. You are all true fishermen and women. I'm more of a birth-control device for worms. But that doesn't reduce my admiration for this Society, quite the opposite, etc .... '

Or picture the faces on an audience of Medical Practitioners as you begin:

'God heals, doctors take the fee.'

And then continue:

'So said Benjamin Franklin and he's dead. I don't know who he blamed for that, his doctor or God. Of course, to many people a doctor is a sort of god, an all-powerful healer with mysterious powers. But, looking around me here, I am happy to see the very human side of professional medicine, etc ....'

The famous American make-believe drunk Foster Brooks struggled to his feet and began, 'How long have I been on?'

At a lunchtime function followed by a lengthy speech from the Secretary, the author Ian Fleming merely looked at his wristwatch and began, 'Good evening.' In similar circumstances at an evening function he might have created the same amusing effect by saying, 'Good morning.'

Whatever angle the Surprise Hook takes – the controversial statement quickly reversed into a tribute, the wry comment on the present situation ahead of your more sedate opening, the plainly off-beat or the out-of-character – this particular way into your material is the trickiest I know and needs careful and confident use. I would never recommend it to a novice speaker. But when the occasion is right and the speaker's first words contain a little shock, the effect can be surprisingly good.

Another Opening, Another Show

Now let's consider some classic opening gambits. Remember this gem from David Niven? 'Tonight I feel like Zsa Zsa Gabor's fifth husband. I know what to do but how do I make it interesting?'

Lord Feldman took that line and twisted it ingeniously: 'This is like making love to Joan Collins. You know it's been done before many, many times. And much, much better.'

Here's another way of using the same joke: 'Thank you, ladies and gentlemen. I feel like the young Arab sheikh who inherited his father's harem. I know what to do but where the hell do I begin?'

Lord Janner found a different twist: 'Thank you. As Henry VIII said to each of his wives in turn, 'I shall not keep you long.'

The elements are clear enough. The speaker is referring to his current situation, the fact that he is about to address us. Compare this relationship between speaker and audience to that between a man and a woman. It's a dilemma for the man. In what circumstances does a man face such a dilemma? On his wedding night. Greater still is the dilemma and funnier if his bride has been married before – more than once. Thus the Zsa Zsa joke. Suppose she is famous for having lovers as well as husbands. Thus the Joan Collins joke. Who else faces a sexual challenge? An Arab sheikh in his seraglio. Should we make him impotent? No, because by implication this suggests the speaker is incapable of performing. Thus the young sheikh joke. How can you use this same sexual comparison to assure the audience that you're not going to talk lengthily? What man dealt briefly with his women? Casanova? Yes, but like Don Juan he is remembered for passion and we don't want the audience to get overexcited; it's not that kind of a get-together. Bluebeard? Yes, but that analogy implies murdering the people. Lord Janner picked the perfect fellow – thus the Henry VIII joke. The variations are infinite.

IN THE MIDDLE

'Expounding your theme' – 'Warming to your subject' – 'Preaching your message' – the ways in which the central part of a speech can be described are generally as vague as those hackneyed phrases because only you, the speaker, know the exact nature of the material you have to deliver.

The body of any specific address, whether it's for a Stag Party, a Fund Raiser, Sales Conference, Twenty-first Birthday, Regimental Banquet, Temperance Lecture, Product Launch, Engagement Party, Garden Fete, Assembly Hall Welcome, Rotary Lunch, Ladies' Night, Exhibition Opening, Christening or Bar Mitzvah, must express in essence what *you* know and feel and trust is right for the occasion. The information you have to impart has to be yours, not mine. And yet the manner in which you convey it can be analysed and perfected. Together we can make sure you are never one of those speakers who stumble along, spreading their own banana peels in front of them.

First and always, and I make no apology for repeating myself because an essential truth deserves constant reiteration, please research and prepare your topics. Know more about them than you need to know. The more information you have in reserve, the more selective you can be about what you choose to say.

Then find suitable sub-headings, deal with them in order and lighten them with just enough well-chosen quotations, asides, anecdotes and personal observations to amuse, inform and satisfy the expectations of your listeners. Just enough, not overkill.

You should never lose sight of two objectives:

1. *What you intend to accomplish and*
2. *What the audience requires*

In other words, attain a balance between what you want to say and what they want to hear.

Keep the Audience in the Story

Whenever you depart from the main thrust to make ancillary points, demonstrate to your audience how each of your secondary subjects is relevant to them. Keep their particular group attitude in mind and find ways to personalise even the most remote issue so that they can see a connection between themselves and it. If people can see how what you're telling them applies to their own lives, they remain interested.

Use Generosity, Generously

If your speech is a social one, return to its human strengths often. Never overlook the four elements of a social speech which are almost impossible to overdo:

Welcome, Congratulate, Salute and Thank.

Give these courtesies generously to all who will expect and warm to such references. If you pull someone's leg, sugar the joke with praise. As the gifted speaker Gordon Williams wrote, 'Praise is a kind of spiritual vitamin.' And Lord Chesterfield said, 'I never knew any man deserve praise who did not desire it.'

It's a funny thing, but even effusive praise need not sound sycophantic in a speech. The same flattery that could appear too florid or subservient when spoken in private seems quite acceptable in a public tribute. Often, the teasing jibe and the sincere acknowledgement fit well together:

'And what can I say about our dear friend Wally Walters that hasn't already been said in open court? Tonight it's good to see Wally relaxing and letting his hair down for a change. And it is a change to see Wally letting something down because one thing's certain, Wally. You've never let down a customer or a friend.'

Know Your History

In a social speech, after ensuring that no speaker ahead of you will have done so, you can plan to include the story of the Society's origins and dedicated aims. If you do, be sure to check up on every detail to be certain of accuracy. I've known a somnolent mob snap to critical attention when a guest speaker made one mistake about the history of their organisation.

Using Humour Without Depending on Laughs

When you enliven serious points with appropriate stories, choose them with ingenuity and reconsider them with care. Does the humorous story arise naturally from the serious words that precede it? Does its punchline act as a punctuation at the end of a paragraph so that you can embark smoothly on the next new topic? Or do you want to use the punchline as continuity for the serious point to follow it? You'll find a hundred such examples in the chapter 'In and Out of Humorous Classics'.

I recommend that you always try to choose stories that have a telling point. In that way, if the tale fails to win a laugh, you can go right on talking as if you never meant it to. Then it appears that your only reason for telling the story was its message. When you weave such anecdotes into your speech to form a seamless flow, you take out what professional comedians call 'insurance'. In short, if they don't laugh, they won't know they haven't.

The Audience: How Big, How Small?

In preparing the major part of what you want to say, take into consideration the size of the audience. I once had to present a plan for a promotional advertising campaign to the clients and their advertising agency. Expecting a boardroom and anything up to a dozen faces, I wrote a very brief pitch with photographs and illustrations that could be passed from hand to hand during a question-and-answer session in which most of my major selling points would be developed. When I arrived I found a conference hall with three hundred people, mostly composed of the sales force for the product. I had no slides to display, no photo blow-ups, no big speech setting out all the reasons behind my plan of campaign and enumerating its virtues. It took all my performing skills to save the situation. They weren't enough to save the campaign.

It could have been just as bad if I had prepared an address for three hundred

and found myself in an office with three. Stuck with ten pages of carefully paced explanation leading to a summing up, I'd have been drawn into a discussion before page two. As Sir Donald Wolfit used to say, 'The size of my performance is related to the number of tickets sold.'

Short Speeches Are Not Always the Best – But the Best Speeches Always Seem Short

Like a good piece of music, your speech has a natural duration. Like music, it may have a single theme or more than one, harmoniously related to each other. Like music – and like this paragraph – it can be repetitive for effect. But if you'll forgive one more analogy, it's like a bad tooth – the more slowly it is drawn out, the more it hurts.

Josh Billings put it well: 'There's a great power in words, if you don't hitch too many of them together.'

The most obvious limitation upon the length of your speech is the time available for it. Establish this at the outset. How long do they want you to speak? How long do you want to talk to them? Plan the content of your speech accordingly, timing it if you can. If you have a tendency to expand on favourite topics or ramble a little for effect, keep an easily visible watch where the audience cannot see you checking it too openly, and try to obey its discipline.

Referring to your wristwatch can be an unfortunate gesture, making you appear more concerned with time than with your message and with the company you're keeping. It's also a silent reminder to your audience of how long you've been talking. Unless you have an amusing pleasantry to cover such a move, it's one I'd avoid.

Knowing When to Get Off

A warm laugh, a spontaneous round of applause or perhaps just a concerned murmur of general agreement – these can often be a signal to the speaker to quit while he's ahead. Never feel you have to cover every point you've prepared in advance. No-one but you knows what you have planned to say, and if the mood in the room strikes you as the ideal one in which to close, simply cut and go into your finish. It's a matter of not just listening to yourself but listening to your audience as well. Maybe the message they're sending you is 'Carry on, we could listen to you all night' … but maybe it's not.

You may have been an onlooker when a performer has reached just such a moment and you may have sighed inwardly when the rapport that should have existed between him and his audience failed to operate his stop-light. I have also been in many a mixed gathering which had more patience with a good song well sung than with a full recital. So keep your antennae tuned to the audience's transmitter and be prepared to fold your tent at any time.

IN THE END

Some speakers feel uneasy about ending their speeches with humour. they reckon that if they are putting over a serious message it will be weakened by a lightweight conclusion. Margaret Thatcher's speechwriter, Sir Anthony Jay, would concur. He makes judicious use of wit in the early segments but hardens to passages of short sharp fact, rhythmic repetition and inspirational uplift.

The American poet Robert Frost advised that poems should begin in delight but end in wisdom. However, wit and wisdom are often contained in the same sentence, and offering both to your audience before regaining your seat would seem to be a worthwhile endeavour. Speaking from experience, I've found that a shrewdly chosen tale which combines truth with fun is a far more popular finale than either a glum proverb, an exhortation to work harder or a declaration of some philosophical principle. Apart from which, there are other advantages besides the goodwill that's generated by telling a good closing story. For one thing, a knockout punch will often make an audience forget a poorly conducted fight and, likewise, many an indifferently received oration has been saved by a verbal k.o. in the closing seconds.

Finding the Ideal Ending

In a speech to celebrate the acquisition of the Channel Island of Brecqhou by the Socialist millionaire, Leonard J. Matchan, I sought an anecdote to illustrate as neatly as possible Len's famous balance of left-wing politics, capitalism and outspoken honesty about himself. Here's how I wrapped up my address:

'I've never known anyone as frankly, fearlessly and funnily truthful about himself as Len. There is simply no better example of this blatant self-exposure of his true nature than this – and I can't follow it so I'll close with it.

'Len had just paid the asking price for his island in the sun where never again will he need to put on his hated dinner suit – that's right, it's a sort of tux haven – yes, he had no sooner proclaimed himself Baron of Brecqhou, uncorked a Jeroboam of Dom Perignon and poured me a mugful when I asked him to explain his political philosophy.

'What I actually asked Len was, "What do you consider the object of Government?" Unhesitatingly and very earnestly Len said, "The greatest good for the greatest number." "And what," I asked, "do you consider to be the greatest number?" And Len said, "Number one."'

As the long laugh ebbed I raised my glass and said, 'Ladies and gentlemen, the toast is ... Number One!' I had rounded off my speech with the ring of witty truth and no-one seemed to recall a very similar tale being told about the scholar and philosopher David Hume two hundred years earlier. Searching through my files of good historical anecdotes, I'd found an almost perfect fit and made minor adjustments. You can do the same. Just try to look at all your source material with a fresh eye to see if it will match your subject. Don't feel bound by factual accuracy. If you take an ideal line by Voltaire and put it in the mouth of the Chief Accountant, it's unlikely that anyone but a student of 18th century literature is going to give a monkey's. A speech is an entertainment containing whatever information you wish to convey. After all, it's not going to be reviewed by any literary critics. We're in practical territory here and we use whatever material answers our needs.

Use Anything That Works For You

One well-known speaker told me he needed to end his speech on an apt line about a Managing Director who never stopped urging his sales force to strive harder for bigger rewards and whose wife was widely reputed to be a big spender. What he said was, 'I cannot do better than end with the words of our Managing Director. Jack once said, and I quote, "There's only one thing a man can do if he's married to a wife who enjoys spending money, and that is – learn to enjoy earning it!"'

As the gathering dispersed, an American visitor made his way to the top table and buttonholed the speaker. 'Say, that last line you told us you heard from Jack ... it's a direct quote from Ed Howe.' 'Good Lord!' said the speaker, 'So Jack's a plagiarist.'

The Top-and-Tail Effect

If no ideal anecdote or quotation offers itself to you, there's a professional device known as 'bracketing'. The two brackets consist of a set-up at the top of your script and a pay-off at the end. Many humorous lyrics and monologues use this trick, establishing a phrase at the outset and then leading to the same phrase amusingly repeated to round off the last line. The great popular lyricist Ira Gershwin loved brackets. In his song 'But Not For Me', for example:

> *They're writing songs of love,*
> *But not for me,*
> *A lucky star's above,*
> *But not for me ....'*

Brackets can serve you well in a speech. The words you will end with are planted clearly at the start, like this:

'I asked the Chairman what he thought was my mission here today and his advice was typically forthright: "Stand up, speak up and sit down." I asked him to elucidate. He said, "Certainly. Stand up so our members can see you, speak up so our members can hear you, and then sit down so our members can enjoy themselves."'

That's your first bracket, set up briefly first of all, then in more expanded form to make it even more memorable. It's amusing enough on its own. It's even possible to use its construction in triplicate by employing it in the fabric of your speech, employing secondary meanings for each pair of words. 'Stand up' can mean standing up for your beliefs, 'Speak up' can be interpreted as speaking up for the weak or the sick, 'Sit down' to signify the need to go to the negotiating table and confer. Those are optional extras, of course, and whether you explore them or not, your opening paragraph has established the nature of your closing paragraph, as follows:

'Let's see, I think that's everything. My mission here today was clearly explained to me, if you recall. (*Consult a piece of paper as though reading your instructions*) "Stand up so our members can see you" – I've done that. "Speak up so our members can hear you" – I trust I've done that. "Sit down so our members can enjoy themselves." *(Tearing the paper neatly in two)* 'Mission accomplished!'

Notice too how the repetition of the word 'mission' helps the open-and-closed nature of the brackets, giving extra symmetry.

Always make the end of your speech a definite completion, not a sudden dismissal or a dying fizzle. It's easier in a formal or business speech when you can summarise, repeat all your main headings, maybe demand action based upon your words, hammer home a slogan or finish on a visual display. But even in a social speech there are useful conventions. You can wish the Society and its members good fortune in the future, repeat your thanks, quote their motto, raise another toast, or even recite a poem. Believe me, you could do a lot worse than verse. Anything that rhymes wraps up an act. Listen, if it was good enough for Shakespeare ....

If you want to finish on a neat, amusing line, I offer a handful of suggestions below. But safety comes first, and if it's safety you want I recommend one of these three endings. For total security, use all three.

Sincerity

When you mean it deeply, return to it, say it again from the heart.

Salesmanship

If you've got an angle, serious or light-hearted, sock it to them.

Wit and Wisdom

If you got the right anecdote to close, nothing can follow it.

'And In Conclusion, Ladies and Gentlemen ....'

What welcome words those can be. Someone once described them as 'a wake-up call for audiences.' If you fancy sitting down to a chuckle, here are some suitable 'let-me-leave-you-with-this-thought' sort of lines:

'Remember, there are Seven Deadly Sins, enough for one for each day, so ... have a nice week!'

'And please drive home carefully. We'd all much rather talk *to* you than *about* you.'

'And please – don't learn the Highway Code by accident. Try to drive so that your licence expires before you do.'

'And finally, friends, if you want instant relief from that dull, incessant headache ... good night!'

'In these stressful times, take care of your heart. With all these transplants, some day *I* might get it.'

'Before I sit down I'd like to thank you for being a wonderful audience ... and you can feel proud because I'm very hard to please.'

'A final thought. Always keep your words nice and sweet – because you never know when you're going to have to eat them.'

(*You'll find a new and expanded list of useful closings on page 103.*)

Etiquette and all that

If the occasion is formal, correct titles and forms of address should be equally formal. First on your roster must be the person in the chair, either 'Mr. Chairman' or 'Madam Chairman', 'Mr. President' or 'Madam President', even 'My Lord Chairman' or 'My Lord President' or 'My Lady President'. If sexual equality is your topic, you may prefer to begin, 'Honoured Chairperson ....' Spike Milligan once did, adding, 'I keep my sex a secret. I do not wish to discriminate against the Sexual Persecution Act. I have not seen the act but I believe they were very good at the Palladium.'

Kings Don't Come First

Second on the formal list comes royalty. The way to address a ruling sovereign is 'Your Majesty', and the correct way to address a member of the Royal Family is 'Your Royal Highness'. After the person in the chair and any Royalty that's wandered in looking for a lost corgi, you should extend acknowledgement to whichever other individuals you consider worthy of the honour: 'Mr. Chairman, Your Royal Highness, My Lord Bishop, Madam Mayor, Mr. Bob Monkhouse, My Lords, Ladies and Gentlemen ....'

What's Bob Monkhouse doing in there? Well, I'm using my name as though I were the person to whose speech you are replying. That's where such a name goes in the list – after the top brass and before 'My Lords, Ladies and Gentlemen'.

And the Rest of the Field

Who else might be there? A Duke or a Marquis? Just add the magic words 'My Lord' or 'My Lady' and you have the correct form of address, e.g. 'My Lord Duke', or 'My Lady Marchioness', etc. Vice-Presidents get a Mr. or Madam in front of their titles. Prime Ministers are addressed as just that. They're used to being called a lot worse.

If the Church is represented, the Archbishop is 'Your Grace', the Dean is 'Very Reverend Sir', and the Archdeacon is 'Venerable Sir'. That's all I know about addressing the clergy because I've never been much of a churchgoer, just baptism, wedding and death. What our local priest calls a 'three sprinkle job'.

An Ambassador is 'Your Excellency' and, as in all instances above, is simply referred to as 'Sir' or 'Madam' thereafter. Having a Knighthood doesn't make you a Lord, of course, so you lump any present under that final 'Ladies and Gentlemen', unless you're mentioning a particular name such as 'Sir Bob Geldof'. But he doesn't attend many formal functions because he finds them depressing. And they do say that when Sir Bob gets very depressed he just hangs about the house, clean-shaven.

Oh Lord, You Made the Night Too Long

You only have to look at the menu of a formal dinner party to see the pattern of the evening ahead of you. Discounting the courses of food prepared without regard to your diet and wines often chosen without regard to your palate, just look at those speeches. There's:

The Loyal Toast

Someone, a toastmaster if there's one booked, will bang on the table and propose the toast to Her Majesty the Queen, followed by the simultaneous ignition of lighters, matches and cigarettes. If the occasion involves a Society, guess what comes next.

The Toast to the Society

Now someone rattles on, briefly if fate is kind, about the history and recent concerns of the circle. And just when you thought that was it, you get:

The Response

The President or the Chairman says thank you and sits down. That, at least, is an ideal Response. In the More Frequently Encountered Response, he grabs his chance to puff up his own achievements during the past year and, unless prevented, kill off a few more smiles by listing those members who have kicked the bucket. Are you ready for your introduction? I hope so because here is:

The Toast to the Ladies and Guests

One of your hosts names the principal guests, saving you for last so that he can describe your qualifications for claiming the attention of all present. Whereupon you rise to deliver:

The Response

This is the principal speech of the whole gubbins, including or concluding with your thanks to the hosts on behalf of yourself and all the other guests. The Chairman may rise finally to thank you, but that's a sort of optional extra. And so to bed.

ALL RULES HAVE THEIR EXCEPTIONS – EXCEPT THIS

Of the many hard and fast rules for success in public speaking, nearly all are hard and none are fast. There is one, however, that holds faster than all the others. This is:

Always Have Someone to Introduce You

Never introduce yourself. Even if you are very, very famous and everyone knows you're coming and the organisers assure you there's no need to announce your name, always insist on an introduction. And don't leave the wording of the announcement to chance – write a short, explicit, honest intro and have it with you. Ask the person introducing you if he is happy with his own words or would he prefer to use yours. Make it clear that this is just you being helpful, not an ego trip, so will he please resist trying to score a cheap laugh by telling the audience that you provided your own intro. I'm sure you can put this politely but firmly. Only if you feel confident that the person announcing you can do it well should you leave it to him. (I'd give him your prepared intro anyway; there may be a vital fact about you that he doesn't know.) If the room is busy or noisy, ask him to quieten the crowd and get them settled before he goes into your introduction. Be resolute on this point. Like a painting needs a frame. Like a singer needs an accompaniment, like Royalty needs a fanfare – you need an introduction.

A BAD BUILD-UP CAN DEMOLISH YOU

Further to my foregoing observations in 1988, and drawing upon a further decade of experience, I'd like to expand on the tricky subject of introductions and how a splendid oration can easily be sabotaged by a clumsy prologue from someone inexperienced.

It's tough to follow a longwinded ramble. It's even worse if you're preceded by some greenhorn who pre-empts what you're going to say because he's already seen the text of your speech. There are some simple forethoughtful rules you should consider.

Precautions Against a Harmful Introduction Are Often Vital

Find out who is going to announce you. If the presenter is an old hand at the job, fine. But even then you should still confer with him so as to be certain that he knows enough about you to make helpful introductory remarks and not steer the audience in the wrong direction.

Ask him what he plans to say. He may have the wrong end of the stick about exactly who you are and the sort of speech you're about to make. A wise host will appreciate your reasons for comparing notes with him.

If his preamble doesn't set you up properly or contains inaccuracies, make sure you have enough time to help him compose a more suitable way of announcing you.

It's okay if he knows a little about your speech – say, its general concerns, style, attitude – but don't let the actual text fall into his hands. I have never submitted my material beforehand since the day, many years ago, when a very raw conference director insisted on seeing an advance copy of my speech. Then this arrogant novitiate stood up and proceeded to cover all my main points, make free with with my conclusions, air his personal disagreements with my views and, after ten minutes of stealing my ideas and my funniest lines, invite me to the microphone.

I was forced to paraphrase, joke as appropriately as I could manage, ad lib my responses to the man's insensitive statements and generally abandon most of what I had written. Despite my best endeavours to save myself, my address was an small anti-climax instead of a big success.

Could it happen to you ? Well, I've only seen it occur on one other occasion when a Sales Director undercut a speech from his top salesman but I'd still advise caution.

You only need to run into one such self-pleaser to learn an uncomfortable lesson.

Following the Man With Verbal Diarrhoea

Perhaps you've seen shows where the compere is determined to outshine the celebrity he's presenting. He may go on too long and sap the audience of its energy, reducing its powers of attention. If it happens in professional entertainment, it can happen to you.

There's no polite way to stop some chatterbox seizing his chance to run off at the mouth. All you can do to rectify the situation is get the crowd back on your side by providing an antidote to his garrulity.

Here's how:

As you reach the microphone, take a good long pause. Look all around you with a friendly, confident gaze. If it's your style to do so, give your head a little shake as if to say with your disbelieving smile, "Wow! What a spot this is." In this way you invite the audience to share your feelings and you measure how much they understand the situation. Let their amusement be your guide. Have they sensed what a bore you're having to follow?

If not, then you may be over-reacting to his tiresomeness. But if yes, turn the circumstances to your advantage.

There are several amusing lines you can employ without openly insulting the previous speaker. Such an actual insult might alienate part of your audience but gentle mockery is quite acceptable:

'Do you realise that, if I were one of those speakers who needs no introduction, we'd all have been on our way home by now?'

Another line: 'Because of that introduction I feel refreshed, inspired, like a new man. It's amazing what a short nap can do.'

Or, if you feel the mood in the room is sufficiently antipathetic to your long-winded predecessor: 'Let me express the thanks of everyone here for an introduction that had all the ingredients of a fine pot of coffee. It was rich, full-bodied in the best possible way – and it kept us up half the night.'

To widen the choice of responses even further, here are seven more: 'Thank you for that fulsome introduction, Jim. I'm sure we could listen to you forever. (*Check your watch*) And I think we did.'

'My thanks to Jim for that generous introduction. It reminded me of the last time I heard him speak. It was at a golf dinner and he talked so slowly he had to call three speakers through.'

'What a charmingly thorough introduction, what I'd call a laid-back announcement. It laid back our time-table by about (35) minutes.'

'I must congratulate you, Jim. I've heard some long introductions in my time and (*Check your watch*) I think that's how you delivered it – in my time.'

'First let me thank the previous speaker for his vast courage in tackling such a vast subject with such a half-vast speech.'

'Thank you for that introduction about which I must say one thing. There were no wasted words. Jim used every last one of them.'

'I must begin by thanking Jim for those brief remarks. For a while there I didn't know whether I was on next or on stand-by.'

'I enjoyed listening to that extensive peroration. Although I was sad to miss seeing my children grow up.'

'I'll say one thing for Jim: he's never gone back on his words. It'd be too long a trip.'

Only you know whether one or other of these leg-pulling lines suits your style and personality but I find they work best when delivered in a cordial manner. If your judgement of the audience's mood is right, the most shrewdly chosen ought to draw applause as well as laughter. A last example : 'Thank you for that kind introduction. I won't say what kind!'

To yourself be true

The central dilemma facing many amateur speakers may be put thus: if a comedian says funny things, and a comic says things funny, what should an ordinary speaker do?

Well, unless the speaker is a gifted comedian or comic, he can take a much simpler but equally effective course to win his laughs – play it straight. Over many years I have observed Lord Mancroft who, constantly in demand for his wonderfully funny speeches, never attempted to act funnily. He maintained a sober demeanour, smiling rarely and only when the moment seemed right. He surveyed the room with a friendly gaze but remained deadpan as he delivered his most hilarious lines. He never mugged or assumed a ridiculous accent or mimicked a character in his narrative or essayed zany gestures. This great humorous speaker left broad comedy performance to the professional clowns. He knew that his best way of telling a joke was seriously. You too can use this approach to rewarding effect.

THE DEADPAN DELIVERY OF DAVID FROST

Adopt the role of a raconteur. This way you can score your best laughs by doing less, not more. David Frost is one brilliant speaker who knows that he is least amusing when clowning and most amusing when appearing to be either earnest or offhand. He therefore delivers his wittiest sentences more like a commentator than a comic and is all the funnier for it.

I sat beside him at the Variety Club Luncheon for Terry Wogan and saw how carefully David listened to the earlier speakers, jotting down a note of anything they said which he felt could be usefully referred to in his own speech. After his introduction from the red-coated toastmaster he stood with a single page held casually in his hand and took a moment to look around him as though weighing up the audience and finding them satisfactory. 'Hello, good evening, and Wogan!' That was his first laugh.

Next came an early chance to cash in on the rapt attention he had given to previous speakers. One of them had referred in passing to Terry's TV commercials. David had immediately asked my wife which commercial Terry was doing. She said it was for Stork. David had scribbled, 'Butter/marge'. Now he continued 'It's a great privilege to be here today and to speak about a man who, as we all know, can really tell margarine from butter ....' David paused to allow a mild laugh to pass, then went on, 'Margarine *pays* better.'

Then he made a gesture with the notes as if they were inadequate for his purpose. 'What do you say about Terry Wogan?' he went on. 'A man who, in some circles, is spoken of as a god. "*God*, is he on again?" they say.' David shook his head as though in dumb admiration. 'Just out of hospital, of course, after a painful operation, having three Blarney Stones removed; sometimes described as a sort of Irish Eamonn Andrews ....' By not pausing for a laugh on the mild Blarney Stone line, David could now take a beat to collect a laugh made larger by that strategy.

Still unsmiling to indicate the seriousness of his tribute, he repeated the name. 'Terry Wogan! A man who spends half his time turning down marriage proposals from lady admirers ... and the rest of his time autographing their bus passes.' Allowing a long laugh to develop and fade, David looked at his notes just long enough to see the words 'Books/income'. Earlier, Peter Alliss had spoken of Terry's best-selling books. 'I'm delighted that tribute has been paid already to his literary works,' he continued. 'My favourite is the one he wrote as he became more and more wealthy – *I Upped My Income – Up Yours*.' This is not a new joke but how cleverly David used it, making the arrogance of the book title appear to come from Terry, not from him.

Having given the audience enough special material about the guest of honour, David could now afford to change the subject and produced the well-tested substance of previous successful speeches. He quoted from 'Colemanballs', and included his own classic gaffes among others from David Coleman himself and Angela Rippon ('I must apologise to the deaf for the loss of sub-titles'). Still he maintained a reporter's air of communication, pacing the phrases steadily and stressing key words with that famous Frost emphasis, and never allowing more than the merest trace of a smile to break the mood. As he continued on the theme of famous cock-ups, he contrived to keep the guest of honour in the frame: 'But Terry's not on this list because he's so damned articulate' – and from there he went on with more hilarious goofs by assorted celebrities and won more big laughs from the audience.

Suddenly David put his notes down on the table. It was a deliberate, theatrical tactic. It seemed to say, 'We've all had a good laugh, now I'm no longer fooling.' His tone softened and his mock sincerity was replaced by the genuine article. He said, 'It's not that long ago that I first met Terry. I was sitting in for Jimmy Young on his programme and I strolled in to say hello to Terry, we'd never met before, this was back in April – and about three weeks later I wanted to give Terry a book and I was inscribing it. And I just wrote inside the front, "To Terry – an old friend in three weeks flat". And that's the way we all respond to him, a man who inspires immediate and sincere friendship from everyone. And so Terry Wogan, the man who put the corn in leprechaun, we salute you.' And David sat down to warm and well deserved applause.

BE YOURSELF MADE LARGE

As you will have realised, I regard David Frost as an exemplary speaker. And I'm sure he would insist that a fair share of his applause belonged to his masterly speechwriter, Fred Metcalf. Fred's put over fifteen years' worth of prime patter onto Frosty's nimble tongue. But my reason for quoting that speech of David's at such length is not so much to demonstrate its excellent construction and content as to show how little the speaker had to do in its performance. If you had videotaped that speech and played it back with the sound turned off, you would be surprised at the economy of motion, the absence of sly grins and assumed outrage. Like David Frost, you don't need any elaborate apparatus to put over a sharply funny address. You can just be yourself made large.

Lord Mancroft said, 'A good politician knows his subject, his audience, his comedy and drama, and the fastest way out. A good speaker knows all of these together with a serenity denied to those who practise politics.'

I would add to a good speaker's required knowledge the awareness of his own energy. Comedy is greatly to do with energy, both energy expended and energy reserved. The explosive clown is an obvious instance of energy expended. But the quiet magnetic attraction of an assertive personality, of latent power, of sheer presence – that's your ace in the hole. Your confidence in your command of the situation is a silent force, working invisibly to your advantage. You may imagine yourself as a Porsche holding back to a perfect cruising speed, knowing you can burst forward into a blur of motion if you feel like it. That's why it pays to play it straight. Cool as an announcer. Giving the Frost report.

THAT VOICE – CAN IT BE YOU?

Most of us are astonished the first time we hear our own voice. The resonant tones we've heard in our heads seem thin and alien issuing from a tape recorder. And that can make some prospective speakers feel apprehensive. Self-consciousness about the quality of your voice might tend to inhibit you. So let's deal with that worry. Let's think about some of our top personalities and most effective communicators, to wit:

> Derek Jameson
> Brian Walden
> Janet Street-Porter
> Melvyn Bragg
> Sir Robin Day
> Malcolm Muggeridge

You can make your own additions to this list, I'm sure. You can certainly see what I'm getting at. None of these gifted talkers make or made the kind of noises that win prizes at RADA. Derek and Janet spout cockney while Melvyn sounds adenoidal. Mr. Walden has the same problem as Frank Muir and Roy Jenkins had – his r's won't behave, if you'll pardon the expression. Sir Robin wheezed and Mr. Muggeridge oozed. There is nothing of the mighty orator about any of them. They cannot declaim like Olivier or purr like Gielgud. When first encountered, they may not have impressed you as particularly expert speakers. But that initial impression can fool you. Very soon after you first adjusted your ears to these unusual voices, I'm sure you began to absorb what they had to say.

What you say is so much more important than how you say it. Great communicators and persuasive actors can make a lot out of a little, it's true, but a speaker without a powerful or melodious voice can register just as convincingly as soon as the audience tunes into the sense and caring behind his words.

All the famous and successful folk listed above stopped worrying about their voices long ago, if they ever did. They are each concerned with putting across their ideas. They speak to us with conviction, sincerity, urgency – and sometimes fun. If you offer your common sense and your humour and your heart to any audience, they cannot resist. The former Archbishop of Canterbury, Dr. Robert Runcie, has said, 'People sometimes smile at my voice when they hear me, but it has never yet obscured my message in the end.'

Rehearse – and make it better

Friends who tell you not to worry should worry you. When they say, 'No need to rehearse, it'll be okay on the night,' that's a red light flashing. You won't be okay on the night if you're unprepared and under-rehearsed. It's so easy and so much more enjoyable, for you as well as your audience, when you know just exactly what you're doing. *And all that takes is time.*

Let's assume you've organised your speech and worked out most of the lines. You've set out your objectives, developed the principal themes, and built in the touches of humour that are right for you and right for the crowd. During this process of speech construction your grasp of its outline and essentials has strengthened and this has increased your confidence. It's almost as clear in your head as it is on paper. Now you're all set to deliver. It's time to identify possible traps.

Now what should we avoid? Well, you don't want to be the Rev. Ian Paisley for a start, so let's not practise this speech with the booming voice of an orator. Neither do you want to turn into Jimmy Tarbuck overnight, so we won't parade the tricks of a full-time comedian. You're not giving a display of elocution, so there is no need to behave like a dialogue coach giving a lesson. In short, extremes are what we should avoid. And rehearsal helps us to iron them out.

Just as in the rehearsal of a play, when the director refines and adjusts the performance of each player, you should listen to yourself speaking your part. Be kind but be critical. Are you sounding so over-emphatic as to appear unpleasantly aggressive? Or is your delivery so bland and calm that it could seem indifferent?

You can choose from several rehearsal methods. Some speakers like to be isolated and unheard in a distant room, with or without a mirror. Others perform their speeches again and again to a sympathetic spouse or chum, either encouraging suggestions from them or requiring nothing more than a repeated hearing to ease away inhibitions.

Getting the Whole Thing Taped

A cassette recorder can be a blessing. I know an expert speaker who is an insurance broker. He tapes all his speeches, his sales pitches and his statistical backup – everything he needs to have on the tip of his tongue. Then he climbs into his Mercedes 500 SL and pops his cassette into the Blaupunkt. All the way to each appointment he listens to himself talk, hears his weaknesses, learns his strengths, spots his omissions, and discovers new and better ways to express himself. On the passenger seat beside him is the little recorder. Whenever he gets a better idea, he puts the car player on pause and speaks his new idea into the recorder. Fussy? I can only tell you it gets great results. And, so far, no road accidents.

If you're taking part in a corporate presentation you may be able to arrange to have your final rehearsals put on videotape. Have you ever seen yourself on a TV screen? Now that's a real revelation. Every dull note, pointless gesture, stiff expression, unnecessary line and ugly stance is mercilessly recorded by the camera. It may make you wince and shudder but you'll learn a lot from it. The playback will tell you about your performance in a cruel way what a good stage director would tell you tactfully.

During auditions for *Bob Says Opportunity Knocks* we videotaped every act.

When a comedian qualified for a recall, we taped him again. If he was booked for the show, we showed him the tape. Shock, embarrassment, humiliation, disgust – I saw all those reactions to the playback. I also saw moments of appreciation for a nicely judged pause or a perfectly exercised grimace. Mostly, after that, I saw instant improvement.

Rehearsing Your Other Speakers

It's worth sharing the rules of preparation and practice with any others on the bill with you. If you're in a position to insist, do so. And if you can record each run-through either on sound or video, so much the better. Let them see their first attempt and then, after discussions and alterations, show them how much better they appear a second or even a third time. Everything improves – timing, manner, content, projection, even an enhanced feeling of importance.

All this repetition and trial by recording also affords you the luxury of cutting out the deadwood. Now it just may be that when you weed out a weak passage in a speech, there is an obvious need to replace it. For example, there's the occasional anecdote that suddenly doesn't seem to fit or which the speaker no longer feels so sure about. The answer: always keep a few good stories and extra lines in your locker to fill in those gaps when and if required. It happens all the time in the theatre and TV studios – last-minute substitutions are made, unclear points are underpinned with a memorable new observation, and often such urgent changes prove to be more successful than the surrounding material.

THE PRACTICE OF PRACTISING

All this rehearsal business may seem irksome but, as I've found to my benefit, when I work hard for the me who's got to make the speech, I'm my own best friend. Enough practice helps you to:

1. Get Used to the Words

By saying them out loud, your mind and your mouth become accustomed to the phrases. You smooth out any awkward juxtaposition of words. You suddenly think of a way of saying a stuffy sentence in a more straightforward and colloquial style. And you can take care that what might have been a hastily prepared text contains no nasty surprises for you when you have to deliver it.

2. Keep Your Eye on the Ball

Running over your main message, the lesser points, the supporting humour, etc., helps to put the whole speech in focus. It becomes so much a part of you that you can achieve the finest possible balance between your written notes and your memorised lines. And you will never lose sight of the ball.

3. Rid Yourself of First-Night Fright

Why do some actors freeze or fumble on the opening night, the very same actors who will bring off the same play a few evenings later with total aplomb? It's fear of unfamiliarity. They're also putting their jobs on the line but that's unlikely to be the outcome of a poorly delivered speech at any function, so let's set aside the professional anxiety.

No, first-night fright is mainly caused by the uncertainty of doing the unfamiliar. The more familiarity with the assignment, the less fear. Therefore, the more rehearsal, the more certainty of success and the greater peace of mind. The actors I've seen standing in the wings, waiting to make their entrance on a first night, may be tense and apprehensive for a hundred reasons. But if they have rehearsed thoroughly enough, they are never frightened. Most of the good ones can't wait to get out there. I'd like you to feel the same. (If you need more on this, see the chapter 'Fears and Fallacies'.)

Whatever form of rehearsal you favour, in private or with a companion, try to reproduce in your mind the circumstances of your finished performance. Speak as you will speak then, perhaps not with as much volume but as clearly and as well paced. Stand as you will stand then, not seated or reclining. Until you practise thinking and speaking aloud on your feet, you haven't rehearsed what will actually happen.

SHOULD YOU TAKE A GOOD LOOK AT YOURSELF?

Personally, I've never much liked using a mirror for rehearsal. It's useful for a dance routine, a comedy mime or a visual bit with a prop of some kind. But for a monologue I find it a bit like talking to myself instead of my imagined audience. You tend to become too concerned with your clothing and how cute you look. On the other hand, I know several fine performers who use a full-length mirror very cleverly, aware of the dangers of vanity overwhelming their better instincts and employing the reflection solely for information which will add to the final presentation.

That said, I still think you should beware too much communing with the looking-glass. It can produce a self-centred state of mind which inhibits communication. But, as I've said elsewhere, try to check your appearance as near to showtime as possible. Some things can always be improved, like that lipstick kiss on your jowl or an unzipped fly.

WHAT SORT OF PERSON CAN HELP YOU REHEARSE?

Because performing experimentally doesn't embarrass me, I can try out new material on my wife or a co-writer immediately and expect to gain something from their reaction. But assuming you're not a hardened old campaigner like me, I think you should approach this carefully. It's very useful to find someone whose opinion you respect as a sounding board but not necessarily in the early stages of your practice. At that beginning period you are only just getting to grips with the elements of your speech and words of criticism can be unhelpful and discouraging, damaging the development of what could become your later strengths. I suggest you get the speech under your belt a bit before you try it out on anyone. After that, the input of trusted and caring listeners can be tremendously valuable. But watch out – they may want you to do the same for them some day. So don't choose bores.

HOW MUCH REHEARSAL IS ENOUGH?

If you were starring in a West End musical you might have to rehearse for a dozen weeks before your London opening. But rehearsals don't stop there. Top directors keep a constant watch on their shows and as soon as they spot a performance slackening or a scene beginning to change shape, they call in the cast for renewed rehearsals, again and again. There's no such thing as too much rehearsal while further improvement is possible.

No-one can tell you how often you should practise your speech but the surest policy is: do it until you can't do it any better without the audience itself. If you have the chance of a run-through in the actual location for your speech, grab it. Likewise, if you can present your speech beforehand to a small group of colleagues or friends who understand what you are trying to achieve, grab that too. A dry run enables you to anticipate the reactions of your later, larger audience, and associates can often come up with the most unexpectedly helpful ideas. They'll pick on a word you're not saying clearly enough, ask you to expand on a point that's insufficiently clear, even add to your confidence with their keen attention and reassurance. If they happen to be in your employ, they might even give you three cheers as well.

Lastly, remember the old test used to judge advertising ideas – is the idea working for you, or do you have to work for it? You'll find that repeated practice is often the best way to recognise those parts of your speech which work for you and those which are hard to put across or simply not worth including. It all amounts to what Sir Jeremy Isaacs once said:

'A good speech is like a good boot – it won't wear out from polishing.'

Fears and fallacies

Asked to tell the secret of his comedy, Eric Morecambe's famous answer was, 'Fear!'

Fear is nothing to be frightened of. It's natural and normal and, as the blessed Eric discovered, it can be used as a positive force.

You would have to be insensitive, inhuman or very drunk if the prospect of public failure did not bother you at all. But it has been an essential part of my Monkhouse Method to analyse that worry and employ it as my ally. You can do the same.

FEAR IS YOUR FRIEND

First of all, consider what danger does to the human system. When you are frightened the sympathetic nerves are excited and adrenalin is poured into the blood from your adrenal glands, two little triangles just above your kidneys. This chemical reaction is vital in energising your body to deal with the emergency. The mum who sees her child run into the road or the athlete gearing up for a race both have this sudden surge of adrenalin. It triggers those symptoms we know all too well – the pounding heart, rapid pulse, sweaty palms – but it is also mobilising sugar from the liver to provide instant energy.

Your reflexes are sharpened and your nervous system with its countless switches, junctions and evaluation centres will use its incomparable skill to channel constant streams of nerve impulses towards the proper decision and action. So trust your stage fright. It's working for you, it's on your side. All you have to do is learn to use these desirable effects, to take and keep control of the vitality they bring you.

I once stood beside the urbane Dean Martin in the wings of the London Palladium. He calmly awaited the music for his entrance with no outward signs of tension. A stagehand looked at him curiously and asked, 'Not nervous, Mr. Martin?' Dean said, 'My God, I'd better be!'

Like any professional performer, he had learned to rely upon nervousness and harness it for his purposes. Some comedy stars I've known have found the fear of flopping on stage overwhelming. Singers and musicians and actors look sympathetically at a pale, shaking comic. They require no more from the audience than some attention and applause, but the funny-man needs laughs or he's a disaster. Fine comedians like Dick Emery and Tony Hancock suffered terribly from backstage terror, quite the worst I've seen. Yet that same awful fear came to their aid once they entered the spotlight. Suddenly the desire to take flight was transformed into energy and sparkle and snap. On a far higher level, the war heroes whose brave deeds have won the most glorious awards have described their own behaviour in much the same way. Fear which might have mastered them became their servant.

HOW TO MASTER STAGE FRIGHT

How do you do it? Like acquiring any knack, you do it with a combination of simple acts. To ride a bike you combine balance, physical motions, persistence and the belief that it can be done. To turn pre-presentation nerves into controlled power requires an equally basic technique that is well within your capacity.

Prepare Everything That Can Be Prepared
Let's assume you have already prepared and rehearsed your speech. Now give

yourself the confidence of knowing that you have considered everything else that could fail you and checked them too – lighting, sound, your face, hair and clothes, any changes in the audience that might affect your references to persons present, the availability of a drink if your mouth dries, all those details that can give you comfort and reassurance.

Some of this final preparation can be done during a banquet or conference while food is being served or others are speaking on the platform. I like to arrive at the venue early and look over it, see where I'm going to stand, get familiar with the setting and make sure I'll be visible and audible to everyone.

At a dinner you can choose a moment to slip out and check your appearance while the desert is being served. Arthur Askey always popped out after the Loyal Toast saying he needed to visit 'the little grown-ups room'. Don't forget to smile in the mirror – that's when you spot the spinach between your teeth.

Concentrate on How Good You Are

You know what you're going to say, you know how to say it, and it's very interesting, amusing, important, and altogether delightful. You are the best person to say it and they are lucky to have you here. Today you will win admiration and affection from everyone in the joint. Believe it. A little vanity boosts self-confidence.

This Is Not a Jury

Your audience is made up of individuals with whom you would have no difficulty in conversing. Now, instead of chatting to each person, one at a time, you're about to save a lot of time and chat to the whole bunch at once. It really is a mistake to regard an audience as a single entity sitting in hostile judgement. Remind yourself that none of these separate human being could possibly scare you on their own. There is no reason to fear them collectively. Unless you are a right-wing Tory facing a Labour Militant Action Group, it's safe to assume that the natives are friendly.

Booze Is Like Success: Both Are Great Until They Go To Your Head

You no doubt know your capacity for alcohol, but allow for its effect when mixed with the stimulation of excitement. At dinners, I always think the initial reception is a danger because there's usually no food in one's stomach and the booze can work faster. Since I dislike the idea of paying the French for designer water, I avoid Perrier and ask the waiter for 'soda on the rocks'. It sounds vaguely like a real drink.

Then it's safe to relax with the wine over dinner, as much as will produce a

mild glow and no more. Hit the stuff hard and the hard stuff will hit back with slurred words, fluffed timing, forgotten names and fumbled notes.

Have no more to drink that you know will help you. Use it to loosen you up a little if that works for you but watch out for that over-solicitous wine waiter who keeps refilling your glass. It's so easy to quaff unthinkingly while simultaneously trying to pretend you're listening to the Lady Mayoress and mentally rehearsing your speech.

As for tranquillisers, they can calm a cough and reduce a tremor, but test your reaction to them on some earlier and relatively unimportant occasion. Don't use them for the first time before making a speech that matters. A Marketing Director of my acquaintance, worried about coping with a very vocal sales force, tried Valium for the first time. Feeling no different after taking two tablets, he swallowed three more. The salesmen, anticipating a top-class incentive scheme, greeted his appearance on the stage with prolonged cheers. He stood quietly and gazed at them fondly. Positive that he was about to proclaim great news, they cheered him again. Tears came to his eyes. 'Thank you,' he sobbed softly, 'thank you so much.' And he left the stage convinced that he had made the finest presentation of his life.

Shoot When You See the Whites Of Their Eyes

Some veteran speakers I know argue against eye contact. John Wade, a master magician and persuasive lecturer, has written an admirable book, *It's Your Turn to Speak*, in which he advises inexperienced speakers not to look directly at anyone during a speech. He warns that by doing this you may seem to be speaking to this person alone and so embarrass them. Further, he believes that in engaging someone's eye unexpectedly, you risk being thrown off-balance should they wink or drop their eyes to the table.

He counsels speakers to look mostly towards the middle-distance, and also to move their gaze around the room, both near and far, without fixing upon any one person. Just occasionally, he suggests, you can focus on someone's eyes briefly, but otherwise you should keep your look wide, taking in the whole room and avoiding actual eye contact.

I really respect John but, in this one instance, I beg to differ. I believe lack of eye contact demonstrates lack of confidence. Looking sure of yourself is halfway to actually feeling the same way. And letting the audience see that you are secure is necessary to your control of the situation. If you feel anxiety, let it be a secret. Such feelings should be hidden. It's not hard to suppress the obvious outward signs of inner doubts: fussing with your clothes, constantly clearing your throat, easing a collar or jingling your loose change. I'm sure you're not planning to do any of that. But how do you feel about anyone who is talking to you but not looking you in the eye? Would you buy a used car from such a person? Or even a speech?

Sir Harry Secombe might agree with John Wade about eye contact. Harry needs glasses to see the audience so he used to leave them off when he went onstage. That way he could smile intimately at a blur, freed from the worry of seeing the odd unsmiling face in the crowd. But John's fellow Magic Circle member, Lord Janner, QC, the former Labour MP for Leicester West and an equally experienced orator, would not agree. He strongly advises every novice, '*Do* look them straight in the eye.' It's one of the many tips on which Greville and I see, as it were, eye to eye.

Opinion on this matter is clearly divided, so really it has to be your choice. From personal experiment you may already know what suits you better – looking squarely at your listeners or letting your gaze roam. Try both if you're still in doubt. But since this is the Monkhouse Method I'm advocating, let me promise you that a more assured and trustworthy impression comes to us from the speaker who is willing to look directly and frankly into our eyes. At any rate, please don't fix your focus on the floor or the ceiling. You may find everyone else doing the same, wondering what on earth is fascinating you so much.

Be Long-Winded Before You Speak

It's taught by singing teachers and in acting schools, but most performers pick it up naturally: it's easy, deep, regular breathing. It steadies the nerves, benefits the heart and, if you keep it up for life, you'll live until you die.

Filling the lungs evenly and slowly for a minute or two is an essential part of my technique for mastering nervousness. It helps to release tension in the neck and strain in the throat. And, as in most demanding situations, it reduces any feeling of panic. Actors waiting in the wings to make that first entrance use all sorts of quirky ways to burn off excess nervous energy – wriggling their hands, stretching, grimacing, bending – but the most common and most useful exercise is easy, steady, deep breathing.

Physically, it puts the world into perspective. The moments spent controlling your breathing are reassuring to the subconscious. The process is so basic to life and your personal security. Perhaps it reminds us that, no matter how stressful the task of making a speech, we'll still be breathing when it's over and done with.

If, while waiting to speak, you are unseen, outside a door or backstage, be uninhibited about how you relax yourself. Use the actor's tricks if they suit you – clenching and unclenching your hands, shaking your shoulders, arching your back – but keep those gentle, deep breaths going. If you are on a platform or at a table, sit back comfortably and deliberately slow down and deepen your breathing. And if it helps you to meditate on something, think about your purpose. Remember what result you want. Concentrate on your target. Discard inessential thoughts and focus on your motive. It's wonderful how this can awaken your sense of survival. And there you have my six-point strategy for marshalling the negative effects of stage fright and turning them into a positive support force. To recap:

Be Prepared!

Do your homework. Research, learn, revise and organise all you can about your subject, then write it down and rehearse it, then think about it and talk about it. Try it out on anyone willing to listen. Check every component of your presentation – your appearance, audience, audibility – leaving as little as possible to chance. All this preparation gives you something to be proud of, so:

Be Proud!

What you are offering to these people is top-quality merchandise – a splendid talk from a very worthwhile talker. Just bear in mind that you are sexy, lovable, amusing – and highly intelligent with it. Why else would you have this book?

Be Welcome!

The audience is not a monster that waits to destroy you, it is mostly composed of decent, friendly individuals. You know one or two may be lethargic, dim, worried or even in agony. That's their problem, not yours. The vast majority of the nice people listening and looking at a speaker actually like him.

Be Sober!

Use only enough alcohol to lift your morale as you prepare yourself – and no more.

Be Direct!

Find the friendliest faces in the audience and meet their gaze. When you've looked into enough interested eyes, you will know that this really is an agreeable audience, a pleasure to talk to.

Be Steady!

There's no need to rush breathlessly into a good speech. A few deep breaths and a quiet moment to review what you want your speech to achieve for you – and you're ready.

BUT WHAT ABOUT THE TREMBLES?

During auditions for *Bob Says Opportunity Knocks*, my BBC 1 talent contest, I sat beside producer Stewart Morris watching up to 70 acts a day. He made notes on the back of each relevant application form, occasionally adding a cryptic V sign. One day I just had to ask.

'Is that a V for victory or the symbol for sticking up two fingers?'

'That, my dear man, is a reminder that the performer in question is a vibrator,' explained Stewart. 'Take that last singer. Good voice and unaffected by the tremors in her knees. But to conceal the shakes she had today, I'd have to get a cameraman with a bad hangover to tremble in tempo.'

'So you wouldn't use her?'

'Wrong. No performer ever quivered through an entire show. The shaky period passes. It just means a bit of extra rehearsal perhaps, a few reassuring words and, if she's still rippling, no hand-mike. That's the most common give-away – the microphone with megrims.'

The thought stayed with me. Had I ever been that agitated when called upon to perform? And how long did it last? And had I allowed it to be obvious to onlookers? Did my microphone have megrims? And what could be done about it?

Then I remembered the twittering flutters that overcame me when I was called upon to speak at the Phyllis Holman-Richards Memorial Centre for Babies. My wife and I had applied to adopt a daughter and we had reached the stage where everything depended upon my making a convincing case to the committee. My God, did I have the shakes! I reckon I could have threaded a sewing machine while it was still running.

A few days earlier I had confided my fears to my old friend, the late David Nixon. 'You have to handle so many magic props with precision, David, you can't afford to tremble. How can I conceal my shivers?'

David said, 'In the first place, remember that nervousness doesn't show one-tenth as much as you feel. If you're slightly scared, you won't appear to be scared at all. And if you're very scared, you'll appear slightly scared. And if you're absolutely bloody terrified, you will only seem to be bothered.'

If you suffer from physical shakes when you have to perform, you can take comfort from the truth of these two observations from Stewart Morris and David Nixon:

1 Nobody ever quivered through an entire show
2. Nervousness doesn't display one tenth of itself

And another thing – nobody gives a hoot. The audience couldn't care less if you fluff a few words and dab your napkin over your brow. They won't notice anything is wrong unless you throw up over the Chairman or have a cardiac arrest. If you doubt this, consider your own experience as a member of the audience. Think back. Can you recall one single speech that was affected by the speaker's evident fear? The fact is that you may have seen the occasional anxious speaker but, because it didn't really matter to you, it wasn't worth remembering. The odd exception might have been when you were emotionally involved with the speaker and sharing the tension on their behalf, but that's a special reaction you won't find in many audiences.

How then, can you conceal the outward manifestations of inward turmoil? Well, there are a few things you can do. And a few things you can not do.

SIX WAYS TO COPE WITH NERVES

1. Take a tip from a veteran TV producer and don't hold a hand-mike if it's liable to shudder. Leave it on its stand.
2. Don't draw your attention to your hands. If you must take a sip to drink, make it as sure and swift as you can – don't hold a glass of milk while it churns into butter.

3. Leave your notes on the table or the lectern where you can refer to them as necessary. If your eyesight demands closer scrutiny, raise them as briefly as possibly and put them down again. When the air in the room is still but your papers are rattling in a gale, then your cover is blown, so try not to hold them up too long or too close to the mike.

4. If one leg is trembling, shift your weight to the other. If both legs are trembling, move your feet back and lean forward with your hands on the table or grasping the lectern. Luckily for me, when I had to address the Adoption Panel, I could remain seated so my wobbly legs didn't show. I kept my hands gripping my knees so that I wouldn't be tempted to wring them piteously.

5. Avoid drinking anything with caffeine in it. Anyone prone to jumpiness can be overstimulated by tea or coffee or Coke before a show. Kenny Everett sat beside me at the Matt Monro Tribute Dinner in 1987 and admitted he was so nervous he didn't dare touch the coffee, then asked the waiter, 'What's the right wine to go with fingernails?' But Kenny, the waiter and I were the only ones in the Great Room of the Grosvenor House who knew he was tremulous. They all thought he was joking when he told them he was as insecure as an elephant's gynaecologist.

   That was because Kenny was a famous funny-man. He could take his nervousness and make a gag about it and no-one suspected that he was genuinely tense. 'Look at that hand shaking,' he cried, stretching out a quivering arm. 'I think people are having a sponsored walk across my grave!'

6. Don't let on! If you are naturally frank, you too may be tempted to tell the audience that you are nervous. That can work if you're a popular comedian like Kenny but I don't recommend it for anyone else, except as a rare deliberate device to gain sympathy for some purpose. The focus of your speech should be upon its message and a confession of personal inadequacy won't help to get it across.

SHYNESS

I read the shyness can be inherited. I wanted to ask my parents if it ran in the family but I was too embarrassed to ask. Besides which, my mother was a very bashful woman. She wore a blindfold to change my nappy. I was breastfed through a rubber tube. From another room. My own modesty grew worse in adolescence. Even when I mentally undressed a girl, I stopped at her slip. Wait! Hold the jokes! Kidding aside ....

Quite a few people, faced with the prospect of public speaking, feel they are naturally excluded from any success in the venture because they have

discovered themselves to be socially shy. It ain't necessarily so. There is a remarkable Jekyll-and-Hyde effect which comes to the rescue of the generally demure. And I really do speak from personal experience.

Finding a Balance

Early in my show-business career I feared that my lack of complacency or arrogance would prove a handicap to my ambitions, so I assumed a more assured manner. Perceptive colleagues quickly twigged that I had a naturally retiring disposition and encouraged me to fake self-assertion for the sake of my performances. Others mistook my artificially confident air for vanity and disliked me for it. It took me years to find a balance between the timidity of my real nature and the firm expression of personality required of an aspiring top-of-the-bill.

But you are not embarking upon a lifetime in the limelight. You need only to overcome any reserve in your normal behaviour long enough to take the stage, deliver your message and make your impact. So what I have discovered in over forty years of hiding my bushel and showing my light should be enough to help you to do the same for twenty minutes.

How Bashful Celebrities Cope

More public figures tend towards shyness than you'd expect. There's an obvious and pleasing air of diffidence about Michael Parkinson, the result of overcoming the gulf between backstage journalism and onstage exposure. The powerful Cockney comedian Mike Reid who hurtles onto the cabaret floor with all the subtlety of a hang-gliding flasher has a very private and self-effacing nature. Commanding actresses like Anne Bancroft and Teri Garr have appeared tongue-tied with self-consciousness when interviewed by Wogan. And Terry himself – guess what? – is an intensely secret man who for many years clung to the privacy of a radio studio rather than face the stare of an audience.

The list of such introverts in the public eye could run to half a dozen pages. Perhaps you could compare us to stammerers whose hesitant speech vanishes as soon as they sing the words. There's something about being 'on' that can turn shyness into boldness as though an unsuspected alter ego were being let loose. The blush of humility becomes the flush of freedom.

It's no surprise to psychologists that wallflowers blossom in the warmth of attention. They will also tell you how often the opposite holds true – that the life-and-soul-of-the-party can turn into an agonised basket-case in front of a TV camera or a microphone. It's a simple inversion of role-playing and those of us who draw in our horns in the presence of a few strangers can enjoy an exhilarating release of constraint when we are given the right to express ourselves in an authoritative situation.

Given a legitimate excuse to be aggressive, it can be goodbye to Clark Kent. Of course, Superman's qualities include moderation. Casting off shyness shouldn't be allowed to expose a raving egomaniac bursting with blue jokes. That's no way to let the meek inherit the mirth.

Blushing

Don MacLean, the dynamic Birmingham comedian, said he took a course on 'How to Stop Blushing': 'They guaranteed one hundred per cent success but at the end of the course I still kept blushing. Then they sent me the bill and I went white.'

If you tend to redden upon becoming the centre of attention, it's worth thinking back to occasions when you have observed the same characteristic in others. Was your reaction anything worse than sympathetic amusement? There's something very likeable about a human weakness as endearing as a blush.

In the spring of 1987 at an industrial show for the dairy trade at the National Exhibition Centre, Jan Leeming gave an impeccably professional presentation, linking the audio-visual display with interviews and voice-overs. She looked lovely and cool, in keeping with her TV image. Every man present admired her. Afterwards Jan joined the top table for dinner and stayed for my speech. I'd been on my feet for about three minutes when I cracked a slightly spicy joke about a topical headline. The gag hit Jan right on her elegant funnybone. She didn't just laugh, she erupted. The room was already laughing but, seeing Jan's helpless heaving, the laughter doubled. Then Jan realised that the joke that had her rolling about was really rather rude. Her giggle came under control but there was nothing she could do to prevent the slow spread of pink suffusing her face. At which point, every man continued to admire her but also adored her.

Blushing is charming not only from a lovely woman. I've seen Henry Cooper blush and win affection by that involuntary reaction to a public compliment and you can't get much more masculine than the man who decked Muhammad Ali. Famous blushers include snooker's Steve Davis, Michele Dotrice, Michael Aspel, Arnold Schwarzenegger, Sir Clive Sinclair, even Joan Collins. I say, if you can do it, flaunt it.

Don't Worry About Competition

Those who suffer from shyness should never dwell upon the supposed superiority of other speakers on the programme. It's hypothetical and self-defeating and, worse than either of those, it's fundamentally goofy.

There has never been a shortage of insecure performers who subscribed to this daft competitive concept. The great Al Jolson used to turn on the water taps in his dressing room so their gushing would drown the sound of applause given to fellow entertainers. Despite his massive star power Jolson's career waned as his ego ballooned, circumstances perhaps not unconnected. Two decades of public neglect were the price he paid for this, until he made his comeback when, though unchastened, he was capable of such self-parody that the public could no longer withhold its affection. Jolson joined Bing Crosby on radio and finally discovered it was as satisfying to be part of a good team as it was to fly solo.

Another American master of entertainment was Jack Benny and he twigged the good-team strategy early on. The huge and sustained popularity of his shows depended largely upon the contributions of support from Dennis Day, Phil Harris, Mary Livingstone and Eddie 'Rochester' Anderson. Jack said, 'People say the whole show's good and come back for more. But if people say only that Benny guy was good, they go someplace else looking for a better show.'

Those who recall British radio and TV comedy in the Fifties and Sixties can think of similar examples, such as Tony Hancock who once floated unchallenged on waves of laughter set up by a matchless crew of Sid James, Hattie Jacques, Kenneth Williams, Bill Kerr, Patrick Cargill, June Whitfield and other unselfish ensemble comedians. The story of Tony's compulsion to prove that he didn't need such support and of his tragic independent descent needs no retelling. It's just another lesson: better to be in a good company than a weak one. Let the entire cast shine; you share the reflection.

Hancock's Manoeuvre

Tony Hancock disliked making speeches, due only in part to his normal reticence. He was a slow student and took a disproportionate amount of time to memorise a script. Besides which he was always increasingly nervous as the time for a performance approached and hated the extra stress of having to be sociable right up to the last moment. But he'd been talked into attending a charity function at the Savoy in 1960 and I was at the same top table when he pulled off the most cunning manoeuvre I'd ever seen. It's an inspired gag and well worth remembering for the day when you find yourself in similar circumstances.

There was only one speech ahead of Tony's and it was given by a white-haired Catholic priest. There seemed no reason to expect anything out of the ordinary from this gentle, smiling septuagenarian but when he rose to his feet and began to talk, all heaven broke out. He was sly and witty and wonderful. The audience took him to their hearts and his slightest pleasantry had the room in an uproar. When Father 'Terry' Terence sat down to an ovation, Tony's expressive face was like granite. Then he was announced and stood up, warmly applauded by a rather exhausted and expectant crowd. Tony's notes were in his fist. He waved them airily, nodded around the room and spoke.

'Just before we came in for dinner, Father Terry and I met in the gents and you all know now what a lad he is for a joke, my goodness me yes. He said to me, "Wouldn't it be funny if we exchanged speeches and I did yours and you did mine?" So we did, and you've just heard mine. This is his and I'm not doing this load of rubbish – good evening!'

The Niels Bohr Superstition

According to that prodigious writer Isaac Asimov, there is a horseshoe fixed on the wall above the desk of the great Nobel Prize-winning physicist Niels Bohr. It has its open end up in the traditional way to catch good luck and hold it safely for the horseshoe's owner.

An American scientist visiting Bohr in Copenhagen asked him, 'Surely a level-headed scientist like you, Professor Bohr, can't possibly believe that a horseshoe will bring you luck?' Chuckling, Bohr replied, 'I believe no such thing, not at all. How could I give credence to such an absurd idea? However, I am told that a horseshoe will bring you luck whether you believe it or not.'

If you put your trust in a rabbit's foot or bit of lucky white heather to see you through a public performance, I have another true story for you.

Tyrone Power was my guest star on the first variety show ever broadcast by Independent TV from the Midlands, back in 1956. As we read through the script I had written, I noticed a coin on a fine chain round his right wrist.

Tyrone's wife, Mai Zetterling, explained, 'That's his lucky charm, that old thing – he's lost without it.' Apparently the charm had been with him throughout his many films and he had a profound belief in its power to help him. 'If I can't wear it on my wrist, I carry it in a pocket or some place,' he told me.

The next evening we did the 90-minute show live from the Birmingham Hippodrome. The audience cheered Tyrone Power's entrance and our crosstalk spot got good laughs. His other entrance was in a costume sketch, dressed as Zorro, the great swordsman. Just before his cue, Tyrone panicked. He told the floor managed, Ned Sherrin, 'I've lost my chain, I must find it, otherwise I can't win out there!'

There was a hurried search but without success and, as I spoke his cue ('Am I not the world's greatest swashbuckler?'), Tyrone leaped from the balcony crying, 'Not after I've buckled your swash!'

The sketch was a riot, but after the show, back at the Midland Hotel, Tyrone remained inconsolable. 'I was lousy in that scene; what else could I be? That charm is magical for me.'

Then his great friend, the impresario 'Binkie' Beaumont arrived, showering praise on us and adding, as an afterthought, 'Your lucky chain, Ty dear boy, shall I have it mended for you?' He held out the coin on the broken chain.

The story was simple. In struggling to strap on his scabbard, Tyrone had snagged the chain and broken it. His dresser had picked it up and, knowing how the star prized its company, had put it into the pocket of Zorro's cloak before hurrying off to assist with another costume change. There was no time to tell Tyrone what he had done and afterwards he had forgotten all about it until it was time to gather up the discarded costumes.

Tyrone, who thought he was giving a poor performance because he hadn't got his lucky charm, was carrying it with him all the time. So the thing had no power. Or had it? His performance had been excellent. So it did work! But wait: he had *thought* his performance was lousy. His confidence was shaken and he had not enjoyed playing the sketch.

It's a curious little tale, don't you think? And the moral is: if you're a superstitious person and derive comfort from some lucky mascot, keep it with you – but don't depend on it so much that its loss will weaken your self-assurance. There's only one charm you should rely on – your own.

Technique and presentation

It's a pleasure to watch a good speaker. Yes, we listen to the words, the timing, the tones, to everything that is meant for us to hear. But the best of public declaimers are worth watching too. The man's stance is easy and commanding, his hands are used sparingly but with effect, and his head turns to everyone, including you. Every member of the audience seems important to him. No-one is excluded from his range of attention.

In show business I have noticed how often amateur performers forget to spread the wealth, sometimes limiting the extent of their appeal to a narrow section of the audience. You may have suffered the same apparent lack of interest from a speaker who, though intending to address everybody, neglects your side of the auditorium. There you sit on the blind side, nary a glance coming your way, feeling more and more restless and resentful. A first-class speech may be going to waste, all because of the speaker's inconsiderate posture.

You can avoid this by matching your physical attitude to the confident manner you are adopting mentally. Stand, sit, or move with pride. People understand body language so let your body's attitude speak for you. Try rising to your full height and then easing back comfortably, legs slightly apart, head back so that your voice can penetrate clearly. Let your head move naturally, taking in every aspect of the audience area. Each person looking at you deserves a look back, just a glance now and then that tells them you know and care that they are there. Don't let someone's scowl throw you; it might be a frown of intense concentration. Concentrate, as you survey the room, on giving everyone a share of yourself.

HOW NOT TO MAKE A GOOD IMPRESSION

Have you ever attended a function where the principal speaker seems to think he's in the dark until he stands up? I've seen him yawn, scratch, stare vacantly into space, ransack his nose, stare down grouchily at his notes, eat like a scrapyard dog, guzzle his wine, ignore the conversation of his neighbours, and generally give the entire room a lesson in unrelieved boorishness.

But as soon as he's introduced, Mr. Hyde disappears and up stands good Dr. Jekyll.

Forget it, the audience caught the show right from the start and they know a phoney when they see one. This fellow's mistake was that he just didn't think about being on display until now.

He's really not much use to us except as an object lesson. Whether you're nervous or confident, your performance begins with your first entrance and your image starts to take shape in the minds of the audience. Be yourself, by all means, but let your best side show. Let them say, 'You can tell he's a gentleman by the way he behaves', or, if you're female, 'Her manner is so charming, a real lady.' We may not all have good breeding but at least we can conduct ourselves so that we get the benefit of the doubt.

PROJECTION

You breathe normally about 18 times a minute – that 26,000 breaths a day – and it's all controlled by a breathing centre conveniently located at the base of your brain and at the top of your spinal cord. This centre co-ordinates all the muscular movements necessary for your respiration. If it goes wrong, only an iron lung can do the job.

Your lungs are enclosed in a flexible box. The sides of the box are your ribs, linked at the back to your backbone and at the front to your breastbone. Your neck is on top and your diaphragm is the base. You use your lungs like a bellow which contains a very elastic sponge attached to its sides. Why am I telling you all this? Because it is your speech-making machinery and you can do a better job if you remember how it works.

Try this: Put your hand flat against your diaphragm. That's just below your ribcage. Now, without raising your shoulders, take a deep breath. You should feel the diaphragm expanding. If not, try it again, concentrating on making the muscle swell against your palm. Okay, now hold your breath in for a beat and then shout, 'Hallelujah!' while exhaling. Use your throat as a tunnel and let the word ride on the air expelled by your diaphragm. You'll be surprised at how far your 'Hallelujah' will carry without straining your throat muscles.

Now try expanding your diaphragm by sniffing an imaginary gas leak. You'll feel the muscle respond to each intake of air as you sniff, sniff again, don't exhale yet, sniff, sniff again, until your lungs are filled, now let it all out with another effortless 'Hallelujah!' By now, everyone within earshot will be convinced that you've Finally Seen the Light. If you want to substitute a word of your own for this exercise, please do. You might try 'Hosannah in the highest' or, if religious ecstasy is not your style, 'Hail heresy!' Practise with a breathy sort of word that doesn't close your lips or impede the outward passage of air.

THE STEVE ALLEN CREDO

America has enjoyed its *Tonight Show* on TV since 1954. Notable as the first unscripted comedy programme to attain national popularity, it made a star out of host Jack Paar and, since 1961, multi-millionaires of Paar's successors, Johnny Carson and Jay Leno. But the first and most feckless star of the show began it on radio and pioneered a new sort of extemporaneous humour; he was Steve Allen.

Allen didn't invent the studio audience interview but he was the first to conduct relaxed conversations with members of the public and simultaneously create original and funny jokes on the spot. People marvelled that he was able to go on TV with the minimum of preparation and produce 1 hour 45 minutes of spontaneous, amusing chatter for five nights a week. But Allen saw nothing unique in what he could do.

We're told by psychologists and philosophers that we use only a small part of our potential powers, and an example of this is the way in which we talk every day. Allen was confounded by the surprise expressed at a man able to stand up in front of others and talk to them without a script when, he reasoned, everyone does exactly the same thing every hour of every day they are in human contact.

When you walk into your office or a restaurant or a baker's shop, you didn't have to hover anxiously outside rehearsing what you would say. And when you bump into a neighbour or greet a friend, you have no need of previous planning to hold a conversation. You employed the natural human gift of communication through language. So, if you can talk at all, your next step is simple – learn to talk to more than one person at a time. All that requires, according to Allen, is experience. The more you do it, to quote Mrs. Cynthia Payne, the easier it gets.

'The trick,' wrote Allen, 'is in being relaxed enough to speak on the air as easily as you do in the living room. Experience is the key ... I do not feel that the ability to make chatter on stage is unusual or noteworthy.' That's what Steve Allen believes. Okay, but he can afford to believe that. He is a born talker and a seasoned inventor of verbal comedy. 'A natural golfer can afford to believe that anyone with the co-ordination to walk and chew gum at the same time should be able to sink a putt under stress.' We, the rest of us, know that it isn't so easy.

But there is merit in Allen's argument, and a wider application which includes amateur performers. It is true that we all communicate each day without fear of failure. Of course, certain persons may make us more tense than others. We may feel nervous when we have to address someone in authority like the bank manager, the tax inspector or the doctor. But it's also true that, just as familiarity breeds contempt, so does experience bring a reduction of anxiety. This is certainly relevant for people planning to improve their public speaking.

You should expand your opportunities to use your normal powers of conversation, voice your opinions and convey your feelings. Seek situations where you can feel relaxed and welcome, whether it's a club, pub or family party, and set out to be heard. If your thoughts need to be organised before you can feel secure when expressing them, write them out – but don't use notes when you speak. Exercise your memory instead. A professional entertainer may be at ease speaking off the cuff but his 'notes' are still part of his equipment, familiar to him from repetition and invisible to his audience. So practise and keep on practising until, like Steve Allen, you wonder why people think you're such a brilliant speaker.

PUT SIGNPOSTS ON YOUR SCRIPT

As you lay out the principal part of your completed notes or aide-memoire, give yourself every visual assistance so that you can easily find your place and recognise the headings. I work from key words written in heavy plain black capitals for the factual material and highlight my joke ideas with a green fluorescent marker. Why green? Too often I have given myself written reminders in red or blue, only to find that the podium is illuminated with lights of red or blue. The marking became invisible. So far no lunatic has put me in a green spot.

Peter Sellers marked his scripts with all kinds of instructions to himself – arrows and squiggles and little loops that somehow reminded him of what he'd planned to do with pauses and emphases. The letter Z meant 'pause in thought', I remember; though I don't remember why.

I watched that charmingly diffident speaker Jack Buchanan giving a speech written by me and my late partner, Denis Goodwin, and saw big purple polka-dots down the left margin. Jack put his index finger on each one as he spoke, moving it down to the next big dot as he dealt with the previous paragraph. Sometimes he changed hands but he never lost his place or stumbled over a word.

I recommend trying this. It can be comforting, after delivering a minute or so of your stuff facing directly to the room, to look down at your script and find a big, friendly number or letter or cross that you put at the start of the next thing you have to say. Once you've found a personal method of marking your words, practise with it. When it feels comfortable to you, trust it. After all, you will have done the marking in tranquillity and rehearsed with it to your satisfaction. It would be unwise to abandon good advice when it's your own.

CONCEAL A BULKY SCRIPT

If the middle and main part of your script is long and detailed, taking up many pages, try not to show it to the audience. You'll scare them. The sight of a speaker mounting the dais hefting a bundle of paper that could choke a hippo is intimidating. In a case like this, I'd break with my own experience-trained habit of never letting go of my words lest some pest pinches them, put the massive script on the lectern earlier on and step into the limelight empty-handed. Then no-one can know how long you're going to be.

SAYING IT SIMPLY

The language of your speech may be dictated by scientific, technical, historical, industrial, political, educational, statistical or other professional jargon. But I would urge you to simplify and personalise such material, even when addressing an audience of experts familiar with the specialist terms.

The success of experts on TV depends upon their mastery of communication. They humanise inhuman facts. They break up complicated details into short sentences and use simple words wherever they can replace long ones. When a statistician tells us that 'twenty per cent of the population in the Greater London Area did not apply for nor was in receipt of dental care in 1988', he is explaining himself less well than if he said, 'One in five Londoners didn't see a dentist last year.' Even if he'd been addressing an audience of dentists the basic rules of communicating still apply. One way is dull, the other isn't.

Gobbledegook

The signs of businessmen's banality are all too paralysingly apparent. Eloquence departs as does simple English. Parameters replace limits. An alternative cannot be offered by itself, it has to be a viable alternative. Your company cannot grow, it must have growth potential. God preserve us from

Chairmen who embark upon an 'overview of our dynamic posture in pursuant days.'

Give the Audience a Chance

There is a very simple rule about local and regional accents. If the audience has an unfamiliar accent, then so have you. Please slow down.

Between 2,000 and 3,000 languages are spoken throughout the world, not including the ones used by teenagers. When the British go abroad without any command of the foreign tongue, they tend to shout very slowly at the natives as if talking to a deaf person: 'Por favor, camarero, uno beero and duo sweet sherryo for the senoras!' It's idiotic but it often seems to work. Of course, the instinctive wisdom in this behaviour is slowing down and increasing the clarity of the words.

A Scot in London or a cockney in Glasgow soon learns to speak steadily and distinctly in shops and hotels to overcome the barrier of his unfamiliar accent. So it should appear obvious to a Geordie Works Manager who comes to address a Welsh Sales Force that he should make allowances for his regional use of English. Not surprisingly, however, other considerations often take precedence and the problem of his alien accent gets forgotten. And if the visiting speaker warms to his subject, he may even speed up until he becomes unintelligible. So, please, whenever you are due to speak to a group of people who sound funny to you, assume that you sound funny to them.

Underline key words and emphasise them, especially if they contain vowels which undergo a local distortion as you travel around the country. You may even choose to make a light-hearted and self-deprecatory reference to your own way of pronouncing English. A Sales Director I know has a rich Yorkshire accent and always disarms his audience outside his own region with just such as joke: 'I was telling George here how the vet had to see to our cat last week. And he said, "Is it a tom?" I said, "Aye, I couldn't very well bring it with me, now could I?"'

But please, don't take the mickey out of your audience's accent. Tar and feathers are still widely available in Britain.

TO BE OR NOT TO BE – WHAT WAS THE QUESTION?

A Shakespearean actor has every right to his pre-show jitters. If he blows his lines, he blows his reputation. The opera singer is fully entitled to a little tension in the wings – her audience knows the libretto as well as she does. But the speaker need have no such fear. You are not reciting deathless prose or famous poetry. If you are ever stuck, you can switch to other words. If you forget the exact phrase you intended to use, you can replace it with another. No-one but you will ever know.

That's the handy thing about language – it's full of redundancies and superfluities. There's always another way of putting things. So take comfort in the fact that you are not required to be line perfect, only comprehensible. When precise memory fails you, fluency will come to your aid. The most important thing is, know what you're talking about. As long as you know the meaning of your message, the words you use to convey it can be subject to alteration even as you draw breath to speak them.

So there's never any need to fear disaster because a particular word or line in your prepared text escapes you. The audience doesn't know what's supposed to come next. Just concentrate on the meaning and the exposition will follow.

THE TOM O'CONNOR TECHNIQUE

Tom O'Connor loves to tell the tale of an amateur actor who is given one line to speak in an historical play. His one line is:

'Hark! I hear the cannon's roar!'

All day long he rehearses the line – 'Hark! I hear the cannon's roar!' – in the bath, over breakfast, on the bus, during working hours, tea and lunchbreaks, all the way home, watching TV, laying in bed at night – 'Hark! I hear the cannon's roar!' – week after week until the night of the performance. He stands confidently on the stage, awaiting his cue. Just as the moment arrives for him to speak his line – 'Hark! I hear the cannon's roar!' – the stage manager gives the signal for the sound effect and there's an enormous backstage bang. And the actor says:

'Bloody hell, what was that?'

And the moral, according to Tom, is a good one for public speakers to bear in mind. Whatever you say is in context. You should always be conscious of what surrounds you in case it reflects upon what you plan to say. Has some previous speaker pre-empted one of your ideas? If so, should you drop it? Perhaps you can retain it with a reference to its repetition – 'As the Chairman has already said this evening, and it's a point worth repeating ....' Unlike Tom's surprised actor whose line was memorised blindly, never forget why and where and when your words will be delivered. Then, when your speech is ended and you sit down, at least no one will mutter:

'Bloody hell, what was that?'

FOUR POINTS TO PONDER

1. If dramatic inflections and motions do not come naturally to you, don't worry about it. Remember what William L. Shirer wrote about the Mahatma: 'Gandhi was not an orator. He scarcely raised his voice and made no gestures.' If the man who inspired a nation with his words had no need of histrionics, neither do you.
2. Your hosts may be reluctant to tell you how long – or how short – they'd like your speech to be. Find out for your own sake.
3. A speech is easier to write than any other written work because errors don't show. The audience will only hear it once and they can't spot mistakes in spelling or punctuation. Few people speak in correctly structured sentences. Why should you? You can be as natural on the page as you want to be on your feet.
4. Don't rewrite your speech immediately after your first draft. You're too closely involved with what you've just written and haven't the perspective necessary to edit it. Leave it for a day or two, longer if convenient. You'll return to it with a much more critical eye than would have been possible before.

THE CORPORATE SPEECHWRITER

This is really a section for the busy executive to consider. Although happy to write his own material, and reasonably satisfied with the results, he may reach a phase in his career where he no longer has enough time to devote to preparing all the speeches he has to deliver. As he moves up the corporate ladder, this becomes a more pressing problem, compounded by the fact that he is now addressing higher-level audiences than before and the importance of getting everything just right is more crucial than ever, and more difficult to achieve.

If this is happening to you, now is the time to look around your organisation in search of a writer. It is entirely possible that you already have someone in the company who could write your speeches just as well as, if not better than you.

Unused or misused writing talent is all too common in large corporations. Your advertising copywriters or house magazine feature writers may be fully stretched doing what they do, but occasionally such specialists turn out to have the additional and different skills necessary for writing good speeches. Your Public Relations Director or Press Officer is writing or causing to have written all sorts of material about your business. Here again this just might be the person of suitable talent to write a speech for you, someone who only needs to be briefed on the message you want to convey in order to compose an effective pitch. Perhaps all they need is the chance to try.

Dangers

Finding an able writer who is keen to show the required qualities is hard. Misusing that writer is easy. You could do it by having someone else brief the writer when it's your personality he or she needs to capture, your natural style that must be communicated on the page. And when the script is delivered, you can have it vetted by cautious aides, who will blue-pencil every trace of daring and dash. Once wit and originality have been replaced with commercial clichés, safety will be re-established and a dozen dull pages assembled by an unimaginative committee can arrive on your desk.

Don't Just Read It, Speak It

But let's assume you give your time and trouble to a promising writer and, under your personal instruction, a script comes directly into your hands. How should you judge it? Certainly not by reading it as you would a feature article in *The Times*. There's a considerable difference between writing for the eye and writing for the ear. Give it voice. Read it aloud. Tape it and play it back. Its faults and virtues will reveal themselves at once. Your own alarm system will let you know whether you have gold in your grasp or crap in your lap. And if it falls short beyond redemption, what then? Where do you find a better speechwriter?

Aside from personal recommendation from successful corporate speakers or top executives you trust, you might consider advertising. A businessman I know put an ad in the *Financial Times*, had five replies, tried all five with the same assignment, found a winner and has hired him ever since.

Calling In the Professionals

If you can't spare the time and effort for all this, perhaps you can afford to throw money at the problem, at which point the best professional organisations will take an interest. There are just a few companies which provide the know-how for industrial shows plus speechwriters. These experts understand the subtleties of spoken persuasion, and they will not be scared to argue with you when they think your ideas are wrong. They spend their working lives dealing in the techniques of communication. And their best writers can put your voice into print. That's what your speeches need, that unique tone which is recognisable yours, not a cacophony of false notes. Just as you would detect an uncharacteristic line coming from the mouth of the

Prime Minister, so your audience can sense your use of phrases alien to your style. It's like Segovia playing a bum note.

These service companies can also produce your presentations and provide equipment to help you, such as autocue and transparent lecterns, so if this possibility appears to you, check them out.

Whose Voice?

I'm not suggesting you accept whatever opinions a professional writer offers. Let his arguments prevail on their own merit, and always show his completed script to your colleagues or your spouse to test their reactions. A good speech should be a collaborative creation in which only one person is heard loud and clear – and that's you.

Say it with humour

The most popular and engaging method of beginning any address is humour. It's that perfectly judged and confidently delivered opening line that both grasps and relaxes the audience. They know they are safe with you. With one *appropriate* quip you have told everyone within earshot that you know what you're doing. You're in charge.

I emphasise the word appropriate. Believe me, I'm not asking you to become a comedian. The profession's overcrowded enough as it is. The point I am making is that humour has to be handled with care if it is to succeed. Each joke or amusing remark is right for certain occasions and no good for others. Sorting out what can go where, and why, is one of my principal aims in this chapter.

WHERE TO BEGIN

Anything can be grist for your mill when the time comes to plot a speech. An attractive phrase, fractured proverb, epigram or verse, a new twist to an old anecdote, an ironic news item or amusing misprint, puns, tall tales, a movie wisecrack or a cartoon caption. The more you add to your collection of such basic material, the more you will have to choose from.

Does this mean you need to buy joke books – those comic anthologies which have millions of quips and quotes in them? Well, you can try, but the trouble with joke books is that they tend to ruin both your appetite for humour and your sense of what is funny. To wade through a thousand jokes you can't use to find one that you can is brain-pickling. Of course, it may be worthwhile. By doggedly searching the dozens of speakers' handbooks available in the shops and libraries, you will occasionally strike gold. But most of the time it's like swallowing oysters. A dozen can be delightful, but a hundred would be horrendous.

Adopt a discipline when you read any treasury of jokes. Limit yourself to a few pages at a time, perhaps a quarter of an hour and no more, three times in any one day. Otherwise your judgement will break down.

HOW TO CHECK OUT EVERY JOKE YOU USE

This brings me to a crucial part of the joke-selection process. To have any chance of success on the night, every joke you include in your script must pass the following four-point test.

1. Do you *think it's funny?*
2. *Can you say it confidently and with comfort?*
3. *Is there any danger of offending anyone?*
4. *Will they understand and appreciate it?*

The answer has to be yes to all four questions. And the cardinal rule of my very first BBC producer should always apply: *When in doubt, cut it out.* I'm all in favour of well-chosen saucy lines. They are usually the loudest laughs. But it must always be the audience that determines the bounds of good taste for you. In selecting your racier humour, you have to anticipate just how they will react. Let's now run through the four points of the test.

I. Do you *think it's funny?*

This first question is about your personal taste. You will always deliver a funny line better if you genuinely like it. If, on the other hand, it puts you in stitches every time you even think about it, you had better not risk telling it in a fit of giggles. In fact, send it to me. Any joke that funny is one I'd like to put in my act.

2. Can you say it confidently and with comfort?

You may yourself have heard an inexperienced speaker who's been told a joke the night before and is determined to jam it into his speech regardless of whether or not it suits his style, appearance, personality, or ability.

I recall a 22-year-old salesman rising to propose a toast to a banqueting hall full of middle-aged grocers and their wives. He launched into a repetitious anecdote about a second honeymoon which I recognised at once with some degree of horror. It required a mastery of accents, and he hadn't got it. It needed the authority of mature years and he hadn't got that either. It needed timing, expressive gestures and practised articulation for the tongue-twisting punchline. The poor blighter was bereft of the lot. But those grocers and their spouses were very kind to the chap. They just ignored him. I've known audiences that would have lynched him.

3. Is there any danger of offending anyone?

There is always a distinct possibility that, whatever you say, you risk offending somebody somehow. Even a vicar's sermon can upset the sensibilities of his flock. The tough part of this question is knowing how to apply it.

Should you play so safe that you omit even the mildest critical comment, the least suggestive wink, the gentlest leg-pull? That policy sounds a bit wet – and could leave you sounding extremely dry. So let's agree that any speaker wishing to employ freedom of expression enlivened with wit must inevitably accept the risk of vexing a listener or two.

Watch out, in particular, for jokes which touch on:

Physical appearance
Political bias
Religion
Disabilities

First, PHYSICAL APPEARANCE. The Chairman and the guest speaker were close friends and had already joked in private about the former's outstanding feature, his big nose. But the audience weren't in on this joke. When the speaker said, 'Yesterday the Chairman celebrated his fiftieth birthday. Mind you, if it weren't for that nose he'd be 14 hours older!' – nobody laughed.

They were embarrassed for the Chairman whose huge hooter they had noted but politely ignored. The speaker then compounded his error. He had a second joke prepared on the nasal topic, one he should have instantly dropped, but the booze had dulled his judgement so on he plunged: 'That nose is so big, he has to get a mining permit to pick it!' There was a silence you could have used to freeze peas. The message reached the speaker's brain but instead of recognising his mistake and switching subjects, he fell into defiant panic and tried to save the day with 'But don't worry, he's having a nose job ... WIMPEY'S HAVE GOT THE CONTRACT!' Groans, calls of 'Sit down, sir,' sarcastic applause ... and the wretched speaker subsided. He'd made an easily avoided gaffe.

Of course, big noses can get laughs. Jimmy Durante's schnozzola, Bob Hope's ski-snoot, Barbra Streisand's beak, Barry Manilow's snorkel – they've all garnered their share of affectionate mirth.

But these are public personalities who have put themselves simultaneously both in the limelight and on the firing range. They are legitimate targets for the comics to snipe at. Private citizens are not.

Jibes about celebrities are usually acceptable, but making a crack about the managing director's warts could be hazardous to your wealth. Leave such insults to the full-time comedians whose stock-in-trade they are. Even the wittiest of personal remarks about physical appearance can sound bitter or bitchy, so rule them out.

Second, POLITICAL BIAS. Unless you are very well known for your political stance and therefore expected to make partisan remarks, stick to a fair-minded and reasonable position if political issues must be dealt with. If you want to use a loaded joke about a Tory, balance it with another about Labour.

Third, RELIGION. Yes, there are some lovely anecdotes with a religious setting and they're well worth employing. But once you wander into the churchyard in search of smart jokes, you're also in a minefield. You'll find some useful and safe suggestions under 'Laughing on Religious Grounds' later in this book. If you decide to explore further, beware sensitive souls.

Fourth, DISABILITIES. Please forgive me for stating the obvious. Of course you already know that handicaps are not funny. But while it's easy to avoid the obviously tasteless reference to blindness or polio, there are some less apparent pitfalls.

Last Christmas, in a single comedy show I counted seven jokes that could have caused personal distress. The straight man told the comic, 'You're retarded,' the comic told him about the bus conductor and a passenger with no arms and one leg ('Hop on, mate, you look 'armless'), and we suffered comical wheezes about a leper, rape, black Jamaican stupidity, male and female homosexuality, and even child pornography.

The fact that this material had been written, submitted, accepted, paid for, rehearsed, memorised, performed to a laughing studio audience and then televised – all this could give it a spurious legitimacy. An unwary viewer with a forthcoming speech to prepare might then be tempted to use one of the cleverer lines, thinking that if it was acceptable on the screen, it would be acceptable from the platform. He doesn't see the post from outraged viewers piled on the TV producer's desk or hear the complaints jamming the telephone switchboards. So he cracks a little joke about the company doctor – 'He told me I was a schizophrenic but I'm in two minds about it' – and wonders why a lady in the audience has started to weep. Schizophrenia, alas, is a tragic condition and no joke to a parent whose son is suffering from an advanced form of it. This exact situation actually happened, and I use it as a general warning to look carefully at your finished speech and be prepared to censor it.

4. Will they understand and appreciate it?

If you're going to face an unfamiliar bunch of faces, research is vital. Assuming you know roughly who they are in general, you need information about their age group, average social position, expectations from a speaker, etc. That master of post-prandial dissertation Sir Clement Freud uses a lovely opening line:

'I asked for a complete list of everyone present, broken down by age and sex ... but, looking round, I see most of us are.'

Once you have an approximate profile of your listeners, you also need to know of any outstanding personalities in the room who might warrant inclusion, the identity of any possible hecklers and, if the occasion is a regular event, how previous speakers have fared. All these clues are a guide to the degree of subtlety or simplicity you can employ.

It isn't difficult to adjust the accessibility of your meaning by varying the way you express it. You do it every time you speak to your spouse, children, to tradesmen, colleagues, waiters, shop assistants, the doorman or the boss. You get your meaning across to each of them by talking in a way they can best understand.

It's the same with audiences. Take the time and trouble to figure out who they are and what they are capable of grasping quickly and easily. If your most subtle joke misfires because the audience doesn't get it, it's really not their fault, it's yours. You assessed their powers of comprehension wrongly.

Using the Four Checks

Okay, our sample joke is on test. It's one from that beloved little comedian Davy Kaye, widely regarded as one of the funniest men ever to stand at the top table and talk:

'My friends, if I may I'd like to include a personal note – today is my 40th wedding anniversary. (*Applause*) Thank you, it's a great occasion for me and a time to mark with generosity so I asked my wife to name anything she'd like to have, and I would buy it for her. I said, "You want a Rolls Royce, I'll give you a Rolls Royce." She said, "I don't want a Rolls Royce." I said, "Name it, it's yours – you want me to get you a diamond pendant, a penthouse on the Riviera, a yacht, I'll get it for you." She said, "I don't want any of those things." I said, "All right, what *do* you want?" She said, "I want a divorce." I said, "To tell you the truth, I wasn't thinking of spending that much."'

Now apply the test. Do you think it's funny? Can you say it confidently and with comfort? Is there any danger of offending anyone? Will they understand and appreciate it? If it passes all those questions, the joke has lift-off.

THE NUTS AND BOLTS OF LAUGHTER

Most of the successful public speakers I know are strongly aware of joke construction. Just a few have a flair for instant comic invention while the majority have simply developed their feel for what makes a joke funny; when they build the humorous parts of their speeches they do so with great care. It's worth your time to do the same.

Once you have a grasp of the engineering principles, you will be able to assemble the components of a joke more easily, because you know its key words and vital stresses, you'll remember each joke better and deliver it more expertly. What's more, this enhanced sense of joke construction will help you to assess the value of other people's jokes and improve upon them. This is particularly true of that oh-so helpful amusing opening. Take these first words used by the American comedian Alan King at a Variety Club lunch:

'My Lords, Ladies and Gentlemen, it gives me great pleasure and no money to be here today.'

The secret of that line lies in the brevity with which one's formal expectations are aroused by its first half and then exploded by the disrespectful bluntness of its second half. By using the normal opening words to disarm the audience's anticipation of a gag – 'My Lords, Ladies and Gentlemen' – and continuing with the instantly recognisable cliché – 'It gives me great pleasure' – the mind of every listener is already moving ahead to complete the familiar sentence – 'to be here today' – but, wham, in come those three intrusive words, placed not at the end of the phrase but within it – '*and no money* to be here today'.

How Does A Joke Work?

I've heard it said that dissecting a joke is like dissecting a frog – the thing dies in the process and its insides are discouraging to any but the scientific mind. Don't you believe it!

No magician could perform a trick without having total knowledge and control of its physical and psychological elements. It's the same with a joke. When you speak the words that make up a joke and the people laugh, you've accomplished exactly what a good conjuror does but with one magical addition. The laugh.

Here's an opening line from Jack Douglas after sitting through a slow formal banquet and two rambling speeches:

'Mr. Chairman, Ladies and Gentlemen, what a great dinner. If I'd known it was going to run this long I'd have *bought* the dinner suit.'

Why is it funny? Because of its construction. Rephrase the same idea and it falls apart. Just as Alan King's line required its comedy tucked inside it. Jack's line depends upon the way in which he shaped it. If Alan had said, 'It gives me great pleasure to be here *today but no money*,' the comedy would have been lost. And if Jack had said, 'I wouldn't have hired this suit if I'd known the dinner was going to run this long,' he might have won a smile or two but the punch would have been missing.

That's not to say there's only one way to put over a comic idea. Once you've got the nuts and bolts of a joke, there may be a dozen ways to arrange them. It's just a matter of finding the pattern of words that suit your style.

Punchlines

A punchline is exactly that – a line that should pack a punch. So make sure you know it. If you are at all uncertain of the exact phrasing of the tag, either drop the joke or have a written note of the payoff where you can easily see it. Don't paraphrase. And please don't fade out as you reach that big finish. Give it all you've got and it will give you all it's got.

COLLECTING GOOD MATERIAL

The Card File

The first time I ever saw a card index used for comedy was when I delivered a radio script to Vic Oliver. Vic was the headline comedian in a hit show called *Latin Quarter* at the London Casino in 1948 and I had been told to write a funny sketch in which Vic would play a Viking called Eric the Red.

His first line came after Terry Thomas asked, 'Are you Olaf the Black?' to which he replied, 'No, I'm a Norse of a different colour.' That's how bad the sketch was. Vic read through it without smiling. The silence in his dressing room was awful. I tried to brighten the gloom by saying, 'I saw Latin Quarter last week and you were brilliant, so naturally funny.' Vic said, 'How old are you?' I told him I was twenty. 'No wonder you don't know any better,' he grunted. Then he pulled out a drawer, removed a long cardboard box, took out a handful of index cards and dealt them out on his dressing table.

'Some men are born comics,' he said as he slid the cards around like a fortune-teller. 'I am not one of them though I've often wished I were. I have no natural genius for the art. Fortunately for me, that's not necessary, though it would have made my working life a shade less difficult. I am essentially a studied comic.' His beautifully shaped hands hovered briefly over a final arrangement of the cards. 'There,' he sighed, 'I've written my monologue.'

What Vic had done was a trick I've often used since. He'd had hundreds of short jokes typed separately onto cards, each with a reference heading. To assemble a seven-minute patter spot for the radio show, he took a handful at random and shuffled them around into a sequence. It needed very little invention to link the gags with some sort of lunatic logic.

It looked easy but, like so many easy achievements, it was based upon past industry. Vic had spent years travelling all over the USA and Britain, working in jazz joints and vaudeville, touring the music halls and cabarets, reaching fame on radio in the Thirties – and all the while he was collecting jokes. Never without a notebook, he had jotted down every funny remark he'd overheard, every smart retort, even clever captions from newspaper cartoons. When he could afford to hire a typist, the entire library of laugh lines was transcribed onto 3 x 5 inch cards and the store in the cardboard box continued to grow. It was just a matter of getting the habit and keeping it up.

Comedy For the Ear Is Not For the Eye

Some of the best performable comedy looks dreary in print. If a critic wants to sneer at a sitcom on TV, he only has to quote the 'funny' dialogue. What played perfectly well the night before looks pathetic in the morning paper. Conversely, written humour which reads delightfully and sells books is usually hapless stuff to perform. You get a feeling for the difference, and that feeling gets stronger with each successful choice – and each misjudgement. Yes, once again, just when you need a shortcut, the job needs hard work and experience. But, saints be praised, it can be a lot of fun, and when the audience rewards your effort and perception with their laughter, it's a great feeling.

Classify and Reclassify

As your card index begins to grow, classify each entry with the information you will need for accurate retrieval. A gag may have more than one possible use, so use plenty of cross-indexing. Take Vic Oliver's line about politicians: 'The only time they're telling the truth is when they call each other liars.' The first heading for that might be 'Politics' – but what if you need a line about 'Truth' or 'Elections' or 'Local Government' or 'Summit Meeting'? The more you cross-index the more your range will grow.

Collecting on Your Investment

Finally, how does the card file pay off? Here's one scenario. You've agreed to speak at the local Rotary. There's a shopping list to be prepared before you browse through your file: where you are speaking, who will be there, who else is speaking, names of previous or present guests, the topics you might cover (unusual weather, current local and national events, etcetera), the range of your speech and its main theme, and so on.

Now you can dip into your file, take out every relevant card and do a Vic Oliver.

Spread the cards out and begin to form an order. Soon a pattern of possible use will become clear. There will be an embarrassment of riches and you can start the process of selection and rejection. Remember, these card ideas are here to support your speech, not to invade or distort it.

First, a valuable line for your opening, now perhaps a good one about the parking difficulties in the neighbourhood, then you'll be into your main theme and will need no laughs for a while, but a popular anecdote to amplify the point might help, and here's the very one. An apt quotation might lead you into a summary of your serious points, then a warm-hearted way of expressing your thanks to conclude, yes, this card will fit, and so ends an engaging twenty minutes.

The cards have done their job, arranged like friendly milestones along the path of your speech. And as their number increases over the years, they will repay the public speaker's industry over and over again.

'A Funny Thing Happened on the Way Here ....'

It's a reliable standby you've heard from hundreds of patter comedians over the years. Often the funny thing that the comic says happened on the way here isn't all that funny and obviously didn't happen. However, nothing survives in comedy unless it works and there's never been a simpler opening line for a comic – or for a speaker. So let's take up a few paragraphs to see what value it can have for you.

Topicality

This familiar formula adapts itself naturally to headlines. When London

Transport went on strike, Charlie Chester opened his Royal Variety appearance by saying, 'A funny thing happened to me on the way here – I caught a bus.' It scored a big laugh purely on its topicality. In 1983, when the world was puzzled by two unconnected disappearances, I opened a speech in a remote hotel in Cornwall with, 'A funny thing happened on the way here – I could swear I saw Lord Lucan – and he was riding Shergar.' So if all the morning papers carry the same front page story and it's not tragic, try fitting it into the 'Funny Thing' formula to see if it gives you a smart opening.

Local Interest

Here's where the phrase can be based on truth. On the way from the railway station to the banqueting hall where he was due to speak, Richard Dimbleby found himself in the company of a very chatty cabdriver. 'This is Castle Street,' he announced, 'famous for always being dug up. In fact, it's a miracle there's no workmen digging it up today.' Richard had his opener: 'A funny thing happened on the way here. I drove down Castle Street without stopping for roadworks.' Applause!

Mood-setting

It's possible to use the 'Funny Thing' device as a lighthearted introduction to a serious theme. Bishop Renfrew did so in a charming speech to the pupils of Dulwich College. He rose to thank the Master for his introduction and then said, 'I've never really believed all those comedians on the wireless and on the stage who begin by saying, "A funny thing happened to me on the way here today", because nothing funny has ever happened to me on the way to a public appearance. Never! Until today!' The teachers and boys laughed at that and settled down, happy to realise that they were listening to an able speaker.

Then the good Bishop went on with his story of how the wind had blown his hat off his head and into the road, a daring lad had run after it and barely managed to scoop it out of the path of a lorry, only to trip and fall on top of the hat. The Bishop's rueful expression as he showed us all the battered black hat was funny and endearing. Immediately he used the tale as an example of the pitfalls awaiting those who are over-eager to oblige and enlarged his theme as he encouraged us all to do good without become do-gooders.

It was a fine and serious sermon but it might not have secured our rapt attention without its engaging beginning. The little incident with that gust of wind and the reckless boy had proved lucky, hadn't it? And it had to be true because he showed us the squashed hat. Well, yes, except that my schoolfriend Roberts Senior was at the gate when the Bishop's departing car paused there and he saw the worthy man sitting in the back with an open case in which he was arranging two black hats – one damaged, the other not. Me and Roberts Senior, we reckoned the Bishop was a bit of a con merchant – and our respect for him rose accordingly.

Openers

Here's a whole bunch of opening lines that have proved their worth over the years. Don't expect to like them all. They are not really intended to make you laugh as you see them in print. It's how and where you use them that makes them valuable to you. And, as I've illustrated, whatever is intrinsically comical in these openers will remain funny in many different contexts.

All-purpose

'Thanks. At this moment I am trying to remember the ABC of public speaking. ABC. Always Be Confident. And before standing up to face an audience, I also try to remember the XYZ of public speaking. XYZ. Examine Your Zipper.'

'May I begin by thanking you for the three great human qualities – faith, hope and charity. Your applause before I speak, that's faith. Applause during my speech – that's hope. Applause after I've spoken, that'll be charity.'

'I make a lot of speeches and they can't all be different, I'm afraid. Inevitably I repeat myself. Much of what I'm about to say to you now I used in a speech only recently at Wormwood Scrubs. So I do apologise to any of you who have heard it before.'

'Thank you for that introduction and applause. You're just like my first wife – you build me up for one minute, then make me do all the work for the next half-hour.'

'Thank you, I appreciate your welcome because I just felt slightly unwell. I told your very sympathetic Chairman that I was feeling funny and he said, "Well, do your speech before it wears off."'

'Forgive me if I appear a little shaken but on the way here I was involved in one of the great train robberies of all time. I had a British Rail breakfast.'

If you are late

'Sorry I was late arriving but I've been at a meeting of the Procrastinators' Society. They've elected me Past President.'

'Sorry I was late but there are eight people living in our house and the alarm was only set for seven.'

'Sorry I was late but I had a blow-out on the Motorway. Serve me right for eating that vindaloo.'

'Sorry I was late but I had to accept an urgent phone call from a woman I once used to go out with. My wife.'

To a large audience

'This is a much larger crowd that I was expecting. I feel as if I'm speaking at a Job Centre.'

'Thank you. I'm not crazy about making speeches but I've been married for 35 years and this is the only chance I get to see if my mouth still works.'

'The Chairman has just said to me, "Would you like to begin your speech now ... or shall we let them go on enjoying themselves a little longer?"'

'May I begin by thanking the Banqueting Manager for tonight's magnificent dinner which will always have a special place in my heartburn.'

'I have asked if I might speak to you before (name of next speaker) makes his speech because I have several engagements in (name the month after next) that I really must keep.'

'Tonight I am appearing free of charge and I think you'll agree I'm worth every penny of it.'

After a leg-pulling introduction

'Thank you. And may I say of all the many introductions I've had over the years that was the most (pause) ... recent.'

After a flattering introduction

'After hearing such a wonderful description the only person who'd expect me to stand up would be my mother.'

'Wife swapping, getting duty-free booze delivered to your home, sex secrets of the Royal Family, ways to cut your income tax in half, and How To Get An Audience's Attention So You Can Talk To Them About (your subject). And now that I've got it ....'

At an expensive function

'What a lavish occasion! The Chancellor of the Exchequer couldn't afford to attend this function. But he's got a man round the front of the building taking the names of everyone who could.'

'Thank you, I won't keep you long. They've found a cunning way to make sure all the speeches here tonight are as short as possible. All the iced water has been imported from Spain.'

'I warned the Chairman that I wouldn't have time to prepare a speech and he told me just to say something off the top of my head, so – here's a short talk on dandruff.'

'It's a privilege to rise to my feet here today and speak before some of the greatest crowned teeth of Europe.'

After a confusing speaker

'Well, they do say it's tough to follow one of (name)'s speeches and that's certainly true tonight. I couldn't follow a damned word of it.'

After a long speech

'What a mesmerising speech ... I enjoyed every month of it.'

'What an amazing speech that was. Although I was sad to see that during the course of that speech, several people left the room (pause) ... married and had children.'

If the audience includes a well-known fast driver

'May I say it's a great pleasure to be here. Now a lot of speakers begin their speeches by saying that and they don't mean it. But I really mean it, it's a pleasure. Because I was given a lift here by (name) and the way he drives, it's a pleasure to get anywhere.'

If you follow soon after the loyal toast

'Thank you. While waiting to speak I've been fascinated to watch how many people present were longing for that Toast to Her Majesty in order to light up. Only last Sunday our vicar was telling the local flock, "It all starts with that first cigarette. That first cigarette leads to the first glass of whisky ... which in turn leads to the first immoral woman!" And a voice from the back of the church yelled, "And where can we buy these terrific cigarettes?"'

'Thank you for your hospitality and a magnificent luncheon. The Banqueting Manager just told me the good news about radioactive lamb. Apparently it kills off most of the salmonella in doner kebabs.'

If you drop your notes as you rise

'I haven't started talking yet and my speech has already fallen flat.'
(For a new and more extended list of opening and closing lines, see page 92.)

Truth is Funnier than Fiction

When you read a statesman's biography or the news reports of political debates, look out for humorous incidents and note them down. Many are far funnier than anything found in a joke book, mainly because they are not artificial contrivances but actually happened. The late Sir Gerald Nabarro had a fund of such tales in his collection and wove them sparingly but brilliantly into his speeches, using the facts but improving their shape to create a funnier effect. He recalled Churchill in his declining years as a giant of undiminished wit. Two new young MPs in the back benches watched the old man as he dozed on the Front Bench during a recess. One whispered, 'I hear he's almost blind now.' The other muttered, 'And I'm told he's nearly senile.' Churchill's voice rumbled out loud and clear: 'And they do say the poor old sod's deaf as well.'

Convertibles

The Churchill riposte provably works best when it is attributed to him. But many other anecdotes can easily be switched from the original source to fit a new context. Take this closing paragraph which America's Democratic President Lyndon B. Johnson often used.

'I think it essential that the USA remain a two-party country, although I've a weakness for small parties too. And the Republican Party can't be too small to suit me.'

Too American to switch elsewhere? No really. LBJ had already switched it. Disraeli made the same joke about the Liberal Party over a hundred and twenty years ago.

Here's another example. The Russian comedian Yakov Smirnoff told me this story about three Muscovites discussing the precise meaning of fame. The first says, 'Fame is being invited to the Kremlin for a chat with President Gorbachev.' The second disagrees. 'No, fame is being invited to the Kremlin for a chat with Premier Gorbachev and the hot line rings and, rather than interrupt his conversation with you *he ignores it*!' Then the third man speaks up. He says, 'You're both wrong. Fame is being invited to the Kremlin for a chat with Premier Gorbachev and the hot line rings, Gorbachev answers it, then holds out the phone and says, *"Here, it's for you!"*' It's a sound story and will work just as well when applied to Number Ten Downing Street or the White House.

Then there's that apocryphal account of Lady Astor saying to Churchill, 'If you were my husband, Winston, I would poison your brandy.' Churchill replies, 'If you were my wife, Nancy, I would drink it.' Wouldn't that fit Mrs. Thatcher and Mr. Kinnock?

Many smart political exchanges suit application to the commercial world. 'The boss of Coca Cola was told that one of his most ruthless executives had has eye upon the presidential chair. He said, "Maybe, but look what I've got on it."' This yarn will serve to demonstrate the quick wit of any of today's movers and shakers. It was told in the Thirties about FDR and his challenger Wendell Wilkie. Who knows to what earlier cast of antagonists it may have been attributed?

GIVING THEM WHAT THEY LIKE

Matching your choice of anecdotes to the nature of the audience is easy when the group is specialised – medical jokes for doctors, religious jokes for clergy, golfing jokes for golfers and so on. You'll find some reliable gags for such occasions listed in the chapter 'In and Out of Humorous Classics'. All are tried and tested.

If the crowd is all-male from various walks of life, you're safe with sports stories. An audience composed of housewives will respond well to humorous tales about lazy husbands, the funny things children say, the nightmare of driving and shopping on a Friday evening and other subjects that concern them regularly. If there are high-profile characters present who are familiar to all, your selection of stories can be based on what they do for a living or for fun, the cars they drive, even the football teams they support.

Help Them to Feel Like a Special Group

You can flatter an audience without them realising it, just by acknowledging their status. It shows that you have a real comprehension of their specialised world. I had to give a speech for 300 married couples in the retail grocery business. Everyone present ran a corner shop. Here's my opening:

'You do look well. It's reassuring to look around me and see how healthy six hundred people can be despite living off a diet made up exclusively from food that's passed its sell-by date.'

The laughter was magic but there was nothing magical about the thought process behind the line or the service it performed. All I had done was take the time to think about the life of a cornershop grocer. As the various aspects of the trade occurred to me I jotted down headings: Going to the wholesale Cash & Carry, Limited space for Display Ads, Having to carry new lines advertised on the TV, Lines that don't sell, Hours when you can't sell booze, Borrowing from the till, Dated food – ahah! Surely customers won't buy food that has passed its sell-by date and yet it seems unlikely that the small grocer could afford to dump it. Then I knew I had my opening line. Rather than *accuse* them of consuming food that might be on the turn I turned it into a compliment – 'You do look well' – before revealing my knowledge of their secret, a fact which most of them would have supposed to be their own personal little habit. By their concerted laughter they discovered that everyone around them ate out-dated food too. They were a special group.

Something Unique Irritates Them – Use It

In every trade new irritations arise each year, there's almost certain to be some source of annoyance peculiar to your audience, and it's just sitting there waiting for you to exploit it. It may be a business competitor who's undercutting them, a fault in their supply service, shortage of office space, a surfeit of paperwork, unsociable working hours, overseas bosses, an overmanned boardroom – ahah!

'Your hardworked management team has a well-deserved reputation for dedication and hard work so you can hardly blame them if they occasionally relax and play a little game. In fact, they've devised their very own boardroom version of Musical Chairs. It differs from the usual version in one respect – every time the music stops, they *add* a chair.'

Are they resentful of a lazy department?

'I must say I admire the honesty of your Public Relations Director. I asked him how many people worked in his department and he said, 'About half.''

Does the Sales Force feel aggrieved about slow deliveries?

'And I'd like to add a personal tribute to Wally Walters and his admirable department which, he tells me, is not at all behind schedule. By the way, next Friday is his office Christmas Party.'

It's nearly always there if you dig for it. Prying for such information may be irksome but it pays dividends when you speak.

Your Very Best Target Is In Your Mirror

Nearly all the good humorous speakers I've talked to have suggested the same thing – before you mock anything else, mock yourself. Let them see you're a good sport. Let them also see that you can afford to knock yourself – it's a subtle demonstration of your underlying confidence. It offends nobody. What's more, if you are seen to be able to take it, it follows that you are allowed to dish it out. Self-mockery somehow grants you licence to have a pop at others. A favourite speaker at many functions is also my insurance agent. He's an expert at disarming his listeners by spiking his own guns first.

'I stand before you, a man who has done for insurance what King Herod did for Mothercare.'

HOW TO BE POSITIVELY INSULTING

It goes under many titles: sarcasm, witty abuse, satire, fun-poking, ridicule, derision, irony, joshing, teasing, good-natured chaffing. The idea of kidding someone is at the heart of classic comedy. Laughing at the boss, at the rich and famous, at the beautiful and strong, that's key comedy for any speaker.

Of course, comedians do it and you're not a comedian. But that doesn't disqualify the use of clever insult humour in your speech. Without seeming to aspire to a new career as the second Groucho, you can win the crowd's approval, improve their mood and increase your control of their attitude by exploiting this simple truth: people like to laugh at other people and they like the person who helps them to do that.

On Your Mark

Let's try an insult. The target: Wally Walters. What do we know about Wally? First, most of the people in the audience know Wally pretty well. Second, Wally thinks he's a VIP. Third, Wally's well-known to be a Roman Catholic but isn't self-conscious about his faith. Okay, we're ready for Mr. Walters:

'It's a pleasure to see Wally Walters here tonight and to share the good news that Wally has at last managed to arrange an audience with the Pope.'

The crowd is smiling. You've picked on someone they know and can see and you've made a mildly impudent reference to his religion. Now for the twist:

'Up until now, Wally hasn't been able to spare the time.'

Pop! You've pricked the balloon you inflated with the straight line. It's a comedy trick that works every time – set-up line and punchline. In the set-up you attracted the audience's attention to your target. You included a familiar fact about Wally to show that you know him as well as anyone else present but you didn't just say, 'Wally's a Roman Catholic.' You made the reference to his religion obliquely and with humorous exaggeration. No-one really believes Wall's got an actual appointment with His Holiness so the fiction is mildly funny to this crowd. In fact, they don't even know that you've got a punchline coming, your set-up line about Wally seems to be complete on its own. Then comes the topper, a simple reversal of Wally's relationship to a busy religious leader; the little man is more important than the great man. Wally's well-known self-importance is your real angle and the funniest aspect of his reputation.

You'll encounter some audiences so eager to laugh at Wally's ego that your joke doesn't need the deception of a set-up line:

'Nice of Wally Walters to spare us a bit of time between hearing confessions.'

Either way, Wally has to be a popular choice of target. You have to know that the audience will enjoy your having fun at his expense and that they won't mind your reference to Wally's faith. Now suppose that your instinct tells you that Wally's vanity is an acceptable angle for you to use, but his Catholicism is not. Then what else is widely known about him? Nothing? Okay then, let's make something up about him, something innocuous that doesn't matter:

'I've known Wally Walters for quite a while and yet I never knew until today that Wally is ambidextrous, which must be very handy for him. He can pat himself on the back with either hand.'

Or, if Wally's delusions of grandeur of himself are enough on their own:

'Wally has a very tastefully appointed office. Nothing fancy – just a full-length mirror and a throne.'

Keep It Friendly

Obviously, ribbing a recognised personality in such a way must be seen to be good-natured. If everyone in the room knows that Wally has just been promoted over your head, I'm sure you'll agree that he probably ceases to be a legitimate target for your leg-pulling. But in the atmosphere of goodwill normal on most occasions where a speech is given, a little witty sniping at the best-known characters present will always score highly. And the more highly placed his target, the louder the laugh.

Harold Wilson was in his second spell as our Prime Minister in 1975 when he attended a celebrity luncheon given by a major TV manufacturer at the Dorchester. Their principal organiser asked me how I felt about toasting the ladies. I said I was all in favour of it, preferably my first wife over an open fire. And you can bet I made a note of that ad lib and used it to start my speech. There were quite enough famous TV performers in the ballroom to provide me with targets but the biggest name there was Wilson. I knew that the right irreverent crack at him would unleash the biggest bellylaugh. So I saved it till last.

'If the art of communicating on TV involves the inspiration of trust, then we are in the presence of its greatest exponent, our Prime Minister, the Right Honourable Mr. Harold Wilson.'

After the cheekiness of my earlier comments about the top people there, my mere mention of Wilson brought a hushed and nervous expectancy. Good – there's nothing like the creation of tension to help its explosive release. I continued after taking a beat:

'When Harold Wilson speaks to me on television, I trust him. He tells me the truth. During the last General Election he came onto my TV screen and told me that if I voted Conservative then inflation and unemployment would rise uncontrollably, the economy would sink into chaos and income tax become intolerably high. And sure enough, I voted Conservative and that's exactly what's happened.'

They loved it. Their tension vanished without trace and they roared their appreciation.

Political Potshots

Quite often we begin to sense genuine feeling behind insult jokes when politicians become the target. Everyone is entitled to a political attitude and a jibe at anyone currently active in that arena takes on an extra cutting edge. There's some real bite in President John F. Kennedy's classic comment: 'You can always tell when Richard Nixon is lying. His lips move.'

Here the bite owes much of its power to the fact that a real-life politician is talking about his real-life opponent/enemy. Nevertheless, the same line can be levelled at almost any politician in Britain today, and not necessarily by another politician, and score with an audience which shares that view of the person's duplicity. Even if they don't, they may well laugh if the joke has a good angle; people like to laugh at authority in all its forms. Impressionist Mike Yarwood, always careful to maintain his political balance, said of Neil Kinnock, 'They do say one day he'll be Prime Minister. One day will be about enough.' The same gag would have worked about Michael Foot two years earlier and will work again when some other Opposition leader seeks that office. And the line takes an angle amusing enough to all but the most humourless of voters.

The excitement within the laughter evoked by political sarcasm is tapped by our daily involvement with today's world administrators and the leaders who oppose them, those who are powerful or wish to become powerful. We often find them rather frightening or ridiculous and so perfect fodder for laughs.

THINGS TO AVOID

Many novices see it as a speaker's privilege to tease an audience. I heard a local councillor address a Women's Institute and try to make them laugh at feminine weaknesses instead of masculine. It was exactly the same uphill task as trying to make a crowd of electrical retailers laugh at electrical retailers instead of at their customers and suppliers. Yes, it's possible to get an audience to laugh at itself but it isn't easy. In the words of the great Sammy Cahn, 'Being good is hard enough – why make it harder?'

Don't Bite The Hand that Claps You

Worse still is when a speaker thinks his audience is a legitimate target for outright rudeness. I have seen it happen with speakers and with comedians, usually the inexperienced variety. Their jokes misfire and they react by attacking the very people they should be stroking. It requires a personality of exceptional warmth and popularity to amuse his audience with lines like:

'Could you sit up in your seats please? These jokes are going over your heads.'

'Sure you people don't have to be up early for the harvest?'

'I think I'll go down to Hertz and rent a faster audience.'

And so on. Lines like these are called 'joke savers' in show business. They can also be 'speech sinkers'; avoid them.

Don't Make Jokes In The Open Air

If the affair is al fresco, dump the humour. Nothing is funny in a field. This mob waiting for you to open a fete, judge a donkey derby, or crown a beauty queen is not an audience in the normal meaning of the word. Out-of-doors is death to comedy. The speaker system will echo or stutter, so anything you say must be slow and clear and declamatory. That sort of delivery kills jokes and, even if it doesn't, you can't hear the laughter. It's gone with the wind.

Beware Repeating Other Speakers' Material

The rule here is: never repeat the joke subject of a previous speaker unless you have a topper. I was told by a businessman of a joke which never failed to win him a good laugh when he spoke at commercial functions. He'd applied the gag to various well-endowed female stars over the years – Jane Russell, Sabrina, Raquel Welch, Dolly Parton, all had featured in the joke at some time or other. Now he'd decided to bring it up to date by using Britain's most prominent Page Three model, busty Samantha Fox. His line was, 'Running your own business – it's like Samantha Fox doing handstands – the overheads can smother you.'

That evening he was waiting to be introduced by the Chairman who talked briefly about claims for tax deductions and joked, 'I'm told even Samantha Fox has deducted £2,000 for her bras – she listed them as "upkeep".' The little quip scored a little laugh and my friend decided that it need not pre-empt his own joke. He was wrong. If he'd reverted to Dolly Parton's upholstery the laugh would have been saved, but his second use of Miss Fox's name killed the joke.

In my experience it is a puzzling but invariable rule that an audience will only find a subject funny once per evening. The speaker using the subject for the first time that night may play with it and perhaps develop it into a vehicle for several one-liners, but when he's finished with it, it's finished for you too. It's the reason why a top-of-the-bill comedian likes to hear which subjects have been mentioned by the comics who have been on before him, instantly dropping any gags on the same topic.

The only exception to this law is the use of a topper to the joke that's been done earlier. It has to be a memorable joke, maybe a story that uses an oft-repeated phrase. Then, if the subsequent speaker can find a way to weave that phrase into his own speech, he can collect appreciation for his spontaneous invention.

The Topical Topper

I remember a toast to the guests in which the speaker told a story about an indiscreet fool, over-sexed and over sixty, who meets a callgirl called Fifi, and in the narrative of the joke, rips his trousers and has to remove them. Fifi was mentioned a number of times and the story ended with the fool being caught by his wife. In the reply to the toast the guest speaker gave his usual amusing speech in which he read out various fictitious apologies from famous people who couldn't attend. As he reached the final scrap of paper, he frowned at the scribbled message and said to the previous speaker, 'Oh, and I think this is for you Frank. Fifi just phoned and your trousers are mended if you want to pick them up.'

That was a topper worth using and the room responded with the sort of happy laughter reserved for an opportunity well seized. Toppers can only work if they arise naturally from something that's well established in the minds of the audience, whether it's a good joke, a bad joke, a widely recognised mistake, or some other event which clearly invites further comment.

By the way, please don't let me leave you with the impression that you cannot profitably repeat an 'old' joke. As Ted Ray liked to say, 'There's no such thing as an old joke, only one they've heard before.' A sure-fire gag is treasure and will stand regular repetition for decades. No, the only 'old joke' to avoid is one that's been used by a previous speaker.

Tops and tails

Of all the many comments that have been made to me since the first publication of this book in 1988, the most frequent have been in appreciation of the useful opening and closing lines I included.

'It's so awkward getting started on the right note,' said one highly placed executive in computer software. 'I want to establish a likeable, humorous attitude right from the off so I've made use of your suggestions and they've worked for me. But I need more ideas because I'm facing the same crowd so often.'

Another regular speaker in the field of financial advice told me he'd exhausted the handful of sign-off apothegms and one-liners in my book and found them difficult to find elsewhere. 'I like to wrap up with a clever quote, something with a bit of wit and wisdom to it.'

The process of selection being so varied, one speaker favouring a wiseacre line with philosophical content and another preferring an out-and-out gag, I felt that a much longer and wider list of choices was needed. So here's an additional segment offering well over one hundred and seventy-five ways of starting or ending a speech.

Whenever a line is not of my own invention I've attempted to attribute it to the original source, i.e. the writer or performer where I first encountered it. I apologise for any inaccuracies.

You may find it rather enervating to plough through such a welter of jokes and axioms at a single sitting. They certainly weren't written or assembled that fast. So it might be wise to take a look through a few pages at a time, lest you suffer from funny-fatigue. Judgement of what's amusing to you and what isn't gets a bit less reliable when it's relentless.

OPENINGS

First lines

'What a warm welcome! You know, applause like that is better than sex and, in my case, it lasts longer.'

'Thank you. And if you're looking for quality in a speaker, I'm your man. People have been looking for quality in my speeches for years.

'I always try to open my speech with a topical item and, sure enough, in today's newspaper there's a survey of British students which shows that (A) the majority are religious and (B) they believe in pre-marital sex. So now we know what they're praying for.'

'Good evening and thank-you for that overly generous introduction. If there's one thing I've always appreciated it's creative sincerity.'

'Thanks. And before we start I've been asked to give you this news flash – overnight, guerrilla fighters have forced out of most of the border town of Ben-umwa-nya-wadi-kaboola-ban-zadi-stan but they're reported to be hanging on to the last two syllables.' (*Wally Malston*)

Second phase

'I hope I find you in a good mood. I certainly am. I feel great. I beat my wife at Scrabble last night. First time I've ever had her at a loss for words.'

'Before we start I must tell you – I was in a big department store yesterday and I heard a little five-year-old talking to his mother on the down escalator. He said, "Mummy, what do they do when the basement is full of steps ?" I hope the questions I have to address today are easier than that .... '

'Making a speech has been described as a game of chance where both the speaker and his audience can both wind up as winners or losers. So welcome to my favourite indoor game. Everyone has their favourite. I know a bloke who lives in Chinatown who's always fiddling around with Mah Jong. One of these days Pa Jong is going to catch him at it. '

'I'm sure your minds are open to absorb what I have to say. We learn something new every day, don't we? I read this morning that scientists say that the human craving for salt is as great as the craving for sex. So you see, all you women who thought that we guys were going to singles bars to pick up women, oh no. We're there for the peanuts.'

'Today I'm going to make myself as clear as I possibly can which is not always as easy as one would hope. Ours is a funny language. Grown people see nothing peculiar about telling a child, "Sit down and sit up".'

'Working out a speech is just a matter of shuffling the words into the right order. My wife and I enjoy playing around with words. We even do crossword puzzles in bed. Mind you, it's been ages since I got one across.'

'Let me begin with good news for all the senior citizens present – of memory, hearing, eyesight, all the faculties, the last to leave us is sexual desire and the ability to make love. That means that long after we're wearing bi-focals and hearing aids, we'll be making love. But we won't know with whom.'

'Before I begin, here's a fascinating statistic – in the '60s and '70s the average number of words in a teenager's vocabulary was twenty-five thousand. In the '80s and '90s the average number of words in a teenager's vocabulary was only ten thousand. This could turn out okay. Another five years and we might not have to listen to them at all.'

'Thank you, I'll try to be brief. Although last night at a dinner party I realised that my wife is the real master at making a long story shot ... she interrupts me.
  'You know, while I've been waiting to speak I've been thinking how stupid we men are. We think you women don't know half of what we're up to ... when the only thing we can really do behind your backs is zip you up.'

'They say you can always find inspiration for a speech in the latest news so I looked in this morning's paper. The oddest item I could find said that research shows that ninety-five per cent of housewives use a vacuum cleaner for doing the domestic chores. So heaven alone knows what the other five per cent use it for.'

'Wow, I feel terrific – and it's really got me worried. My doctor says, at my age, I shouldn't feel this good.'

'Aren't statistics amazing? According to a survey in today's paper only thirty-nine per cent of husbands prefer making love to going to a football match. And eighty-three per cent of wives prefer making love when their husbands are at a football match. Now me, all I'm after is one hundred per cent of your attention for a very small percentage of your time ....'

'I wouldn't be standing here unless I believed I have some really good advice to offer you. And good advice is like money in the bank. Of course, in turn, money in the bank's a bit like toothpaste – easy to get it out, very hard to put it back. There used to be a popular expression: "Money talks." Can you imagine what a fifty pence piece would say these days? "Hi, I'm fifty p.! I'm not on speaking terms with the butcher; I'm too small to buy a litre of petrol; I can't afford a tub of popcorn in the cinema; I'm not big enough to buy you a pint; but hey, on Sunday in the collection box, I'm considered a big deal!"'

'Today I'll be speaking to you in English which is a lot easier than spelling it. Heaven knows, English isn't the easiest language to spell. Take O.U.G.H., how do you pronounce it ? Last night I went to bed early with a chesty cough, C.O.U.G.H., cough. But the town is called Slough, and a tree has a bough and a farmer uses a plough – so who knows? Maybe I went to bed early with a chesty cow.'

'Thank you. More worrying news in today's papers – it seems that forty-five thousand of the country's adults can't read simple street names. I'd no idea we'd got that many postmen, had you?' (*Debbie Barham*)

'Welcome to all you playful people and I hope you're in the mood to play the game with me. It's called speechifying. I do the hard part which is talking and you do the easy part, pretending to listen. Games are fun for everyone, aren't they? My wife enjoys cards, for years now she's played poker with the girls once a week. In fact, that's how she got me – one night, she lost. I always enjoy board games – chess, Scrabble, and now there's the new modernised Government Monopoly. It's the same as ordinary Monopoly but you borrow the money from another game.'

'Thank you. More crime statistics in today's paper – they show that your car is most likely to be stolen while it's parked in front of your house. Well, I'm a bit too smart for that ... I park it in front of my neighbour's house.'

'I rise to address you on an historic day – the birthday in 1834 of James Whistler who became famous for painting his mother. Which was okay by her. What she hated was cleaning it off herself afterwards with a wire brush.'

'You all look very well which cheers me up for a start. I do appreciate smiling faces. There was a lovely photo in the paper this morning, did you see it ? A very proud young mother who, nine months ago, took a saccharin instead of the Pill and has just had the sweetest baby. Aaaah!'

'Speaking to an audience that knows as much about the subject as the speaker is quite daunting. It's like a game of chess where a wrong move is fatal. But chess also has its lighter aspects. I've just read about a glamorous art student who carves chess pieces. She charges ten pounds for a pawn, twenty pounds for a bishop and a hundred pounds for the knight, which I think is a rook. Anyway, here's my opening gambit ....'

'In preparing my speech for you I found myself throroughly enjoying the game of choosing the right words to make the right connections, almost the verbal equivalent of playing Scrabble. That comparison came to mind because I read today that doctors say there's no need to operate on the man who swallowed all the tiles from his Scrabble set. They say the problem will eventually work itself out but not in so many words.' (*Ronnie Barker*)

'I hope you're ready for this. I hope *I'm* ready for this. In this fast-moving world it's important to be ready for anything. My brother carries his darts everywhere with him, just on the off-chance that he might come across a traffic warden bending down to tie his bootlaces.'

'I hope you like this speech I've prepared, I read it to my dog last night and he seemed to like it. And he's a smart dog. Oh yes, I've even trained him to play poker with me although he's pretty easy to beat because, whenever he has a good hand, his tail wags.'

'I'm told that after-dinner speaking is fast becoming one of the nation's favourite spectator sports. And you know, our favourite sports didn't develop without sacrifice. Take my poor uncle Benedict, he was the tragic sports fanatic who spent his life inventing a game vaguely similar to cricket and then discovered that England had been playing it for years. It's certainly a game that'll get you into a lot less trouble at home than a jigsaw puzzle. Only the other week the world's greatest jigsaw designer was divorced when his wife found out he was keeping a piece on the side.'

'It's been said that the chances of correctly predicting how a speech will go down are a bit like playing a slot machine. Of course, the trouble with hitting the jackpot in a slot machine is it takes so long to put it all back. I just hope you'll think I'm coming up with a few winning lines.'

'Today I'll be addressing some tricky problems. But then life is full of difficult questions, isn't it? Like, if Concorde is faster than sound, why can I phone New York faster than I can fly there?'

'Today I'll be offering you some answers to questions you may not have asked. Sometimes coming up with a right answer helps you to recognise the existence of a problem of which you were unaware. Have you ever tried that with riddles? For instance, the answer is "Who, me?" and the question is, "Can you name two English pronouns?"

Here's a classic schoolboy's example of that: the answer is "His last one" – and the question is, "In which battle did Nelson die?"

Again, the answer might be "A Get Well card" and the question: "What does a sadist send to a hypochondriac?"

Another daft example: the answer is "Bombay". The question is, "In what part of an aeroplane is it inadvisable to fall asleep?"

Here's an answer for you, what's the question? The answer is "Send in the Clowns". Okay, and the question is "How does the Prime Minister start a Cabinet meeting?"

Of course, there are some questions for which there are no answers – like, if cleanliness is next to Godliness, how is it you don't find more soap at Baptisms?' (There are more unanswerable questions in *Over the Limit*, my second book of memoirs.)

'Before I get started I've been asked to give you this news flash – the army expedition into the jungles of New Guinea to suppress cannibalism in the region has suffered a setback. Cannibals have already had three hard-boiled sergeants, two half-baked corporals and a raw recruit.' (*The Two Ronnies*)

'I don't know how many of you know this but we meet on an historic anniversary. For it was on this day in 1912 that South Pole explorer Captain Scott of the Antarctic told his men, "I don't care how lonely it gets down here, you can't bring a penguin into the tent and call her Valerie."'

'Thank you for your kind applause. My paternal grandfather once said this about kindness : kindness is a language the deaf can hear and the blind can see. So tell you what – I'll be the kind who's kind to you if you'll kindly be the same kind to me.'

'Public speaking is a sort of game. We're a game-loving nation – every summer across the land you can hear the evocative sound of leather striking willow –

a golfer kicking a tree that's in the way. We British, we have hearts of oak and heads to match. There's nowhere like the good old British seaside where you can roll up your trousers, take off your shirt and go for a paddle – and the men can do the same. So let's get game-playing.'

'Composing a speech has its pitfalls. The English language has so many rare words and double meanings, like only yesterday my wife and I were going out and I said, "Hey, you don't look too bad in that beigy brown colour." She said, "Fawn." So I said (fawning), "Oooh, but you're a vision of beauty in that exquisite shade, beloved!"'

If you have a cold

'I'm sorry if I sound a bit stuffy today. I phoned the doctor this morning, I said, "I'm Bob Monkhouse and I think I've got the flu." He said, "I'm sorry, there's no known cure for either of those conditions." I haven't any faith in the man anyway, all his patients are ill.'

'I have the great pleasure of attending many functions and I'm often asked how I relax after the excitement, the pressure of formal occasions and noisy glamour of banquets. Well, I go straight home to where I live, my little house – next to the woods and the wild creatures. Not quite as peaceful as it sounds, I'm afraid. The Woods have fifteen kids and the Wild Creatures are a heavy metal band. Fortunately we have a holiday home, just two bedrooms, ours and a guest bedroom which is small but it's big enough for visiting relatives to be comfortable. So we're making that smaller.'

If you have notes

'Forgive my using notes but lately I can't trust my memory as well as I used to. The entertainer Barry Cryer says the one good thing about loss of memory is that every ten minutes or so you get a whole new circle of friends.'

'My task now is to be honest with you. Not always easy. I read the other day that the average person tells one hundred and eighty lies every day. That's not much but we can't all be politicians.'

If the company is foreign-owned

'Despite the origins of this great company, the UK division is encouraged to play to its national strengths. The comedian Ted Rogers said on TV recently that we've got to think British but how can we? You come home and your spouse waves through the Venetian blinds, greets you at the French window with the Afghan hound and the Siamese cat, sits you down to a meal of hamburger, frankfurters, swedes and brussel sprouts followed by Danish pastry or Swiss roll and then says, "Let's eat out tomorrow" ... "Who's going to pay?" ... "We'll go Dutch!"'

'I'm delighted to be here to speak to you on this historical date. In America, today is National Forest Day and a forest can come in very handy especially if you want to hide a tree.'

If you're wearing a lounge suit at a black-tie function

'I apologise for being improperly turned out for this occasion. Does this suit look clean enough? The sign in the dry cleaners' window said: "JOSEPH JONES, DRY CLEANER – IN BY TEN, OUT BY FIVE". I took my suits in at ten and I said, "Can I have these back by five?" He said, "These won't be ready till Friday." I said, "But, Mr Jones, your sign says 'IN BY TEN, OUT BY FIVE'," and he said, "That's me!"'

If the function is running late

'I promise I won't keep you too long. I always keep a eye on my timing. We should be grateful for watches and clocks, at least we know when to be somewhere. In prehistoric days they had no time-keeping devices. How could you be on time to keep a date in those days? You'd show up to meet your friend outside her cave .... "Where've you been? You were supposed to be here before!" ... "I didn't say I'd be here before, I said I would be here later, it's barely now, I'm early!"'

If you're going to use technical or ambiguous terms

'Before I start on my subject today, it's necessary for me to define some of the terms I'll be using. Please don't be alarmed, some definitions can be fun. Here are a few that might amuse you. Recycling: a mosquito biting Dracula. Redundancy: crossing a homing pigeon with a boomerang. Alimony: a splitting headache. Just time for two more – Judiciary: where an Israeli does the washing up. And finally, from my eight-year-old god-daughter, cement: stuff that won't set till a dog's run across it.'

'I make a lot of speeches to audiences of all kinds and some people react to what I say in curious ways. They get so excited. One woman phoned me up because I hadn't replied to her. She said, "Mr Monkhouse, did you get my letter saying I found your attitude sleazy and lecherous, your attempts at humour pathetic and your general demeanour vile in the extreme?" I said,

"No, madam, I got your letter saying that my words were well-chosen, wise and inspirational." And she said, "Oh my God! I must phone the vicar."'

'My subject tonight is basically a serious one and I intend to treat it seriously. But not entirely. You can find fun in the unlikeliest places, even the graveyard. I saw one epitaph in our village church cemetery: "Here lies window-cleaner Marcus Burke, who alas stepped back to admire his work." A Welsh friend of mine sent me this one: "Wherever you be, let your wind go free ... for keeping it in was the death of Bryn." And I'm told that when a Theodore Myer died in New Jersey, his widow had the headstone engraved, "The light of my life has gone out." But when she remarried a year later she added, "I just found another match!"'

'I often wonder who's more nervous before a speech – the speaker or the audience. People often ask me whether I suffer from nerves. Well, don't we all? I used to be frightened of everything – scared of flying, scared of animals, scared of crowds – so I went to see a hypnotist. Now I'm scared of eyes. But your warm reception has banished my every trepidation ....'

If you're speaking to senior citizens

'They tell me we have a few citizens here who are in their late seventies and eighties but then that's not really old, is it? There's a gravestone in our village for a lady who lived to be a hundred and ten – a Mrs Lawson from Aylesbury. And I saw another stone once in Scotland for a chap who lived to be two hundred and fifty. Two hundred and fifty! Some fellow called Miles from London.'

If you're going to quote surprising facts and figures

'I'm going to state some facts that may surprise you but I assure you that everything I say has been thoroughly researched and checked. Aren't we funny people? If you tell someone that there are two hundred and eighty-nine billion, four thousand and seventy-six thousand, five hundred and thirty-seven visible stars in the sky, they'll believe you. But if you show 'em a sign that says "wet paint", they always have to check.'

'Welcome to my kind of sport, the sort where we exercise our imaginations and jump to conclusions. People get so excited about the more dangerous sports, don't they? Like motor racing – all the champagne, the kissing and hugging, and then the flashbulbs going off. Big deal ... I remember being caught in a dozen hotel rooms that were like that.'

'I'm about to deliver what you might call a fact-ogram combined with what I hope will also be a fun-ogram. They're all the rage still, aren't they, kissograms, stripograms? My wife and I had a blazing row at home last week and she sent me an anagram. Yes, her brother came round and completely rearranged me.'

'You know, if you and I each have a penny and we exchange pennies, you'd still only have one penny and I'd still only have one penny. But if you have an idea and I have an idea and we exchange ideas, you'd now have two ideas and I'd now have two ideas.

'If my speech today seems lighthearted, well, most of us could do with a spot of harmless fun in these often difficult times we live in. Not like in Ancient Rome where their idea of a spectator sport was throwing Christians to the lions. Of course when the Romans invaded Britain we hadn't got any lions so they threw Christians to the sheep. It didn't kill them but they were badly grazed. Cheer up! After that one the jokes can only get better ....'

If you're speaking for the first time

'This is the first time I've ever given a speech so I hope you'll excuse my failings. I take some comfort from the fact that no-one achieves perfection with a first attempt. After a concert a fan rushed up to the famous violinist Fritz Kreisler and gushed, "I'd give my whole life to play as beautifully as you do." Kreisler replied, "I did."'

If you quote a survey result or statistic

'That's if you can believe these surveys. I read one that said seventy per cent of British married couples would rather eat a good meal in a restaurant than have sex. That's because it might disturb the people at the other tables I expect.'

'Well, that's according to the current surveys and, goodness me, those things can be fascinating. They've found out that the average man speaks twenty-five thousand words a day. And the average woman speaks thirty thousand. Unfortunately when I get home at night I've spoken my twenty-five thousand and my wife hasn't started on her thirty thousand.'

If you want to kid about someone present

Before I get going I must tell you – yesterday was your Chairman's birthday and somehow he got wind of the fact that we'd hired a Strippogram to surprise him. Last night in the pub he tore all the clothes off this woman dressed as a traffic warden. Then the real stripper came in dressed as a nun and said, "Sorry I'm late." But he'd been towed away by then. And clamped.'

'The comedian Les Dawson always used to say that an old pro can tell instantly whether the audience is going to be kind or cruel. (*Pause for mild reaction*) So all that's left for me to say is, "Hallo, welcome to this delightful occasion and Heil Hitler."'

'I'm in a great mood this evening. I only hope you're all feeling as good as me, all my aches and pains are but a memory now, ever since I found this voodoo acupuncturist. You don't have to go. He just uses a little doll that looks like you. And you'll just be walking along the street and all of a sudden you go, (*Give a wriggle*) "Ooh, that's much better!"'

'Today the chairman told me to just relax and be myself. but, hey, that's how I lost my last job.'

'Public speaking takes me all over this wonderful country of ours. I think there's nowhere like Britain for a break. I told my wife, "Next Spring I've arranged for us to go the Lake District and take a cottage." She said, "Do we need to? Surely there are some already there." I didn't argue.'

'May I begin by saying that, as a public speaker, I have a strict policy of absolutely no cursing, sex or violence. So just knock it off for twenty minutes and listen to me instead.'

'I'm told that speaking in public as much as I do can cause exhaustion of the lingual muscles or "speaker's tongue". It was in a list of new complaints that doctors have to deal with. The others were squash player's wrist, weightlifter's elbow, jogger's nipples, frisbee flinger's fingers, Walkman ears and computer operator's eyeballs. Sounds like a fast food menu for cannibals, doesn't it?'

'Thank you. I must say that so far this event has gone exactly as the chairman said it would. He said, "Bob, this evening is going to have flair, pace, wit, quality – and then you come on."'

'I know that I'm speaking to a well-organised group. Which brings to mind the wise words from the American humourist Robert Orben who says the most efficient part of any organisation is a standing committee. The minute you give them chairs, the meetings last forever.'

'Before I begin I must warn you that parts of this speech may be unsuitable for persons of a nervous disposition – "Boo!!" that was one of the parts.'

'Thank you. And to begin, here's a message for anyone here who happens to be a clairvoyant, astrologer, crystal-ball gazer or tea-cup reader. I do hope you've enjoyed my speech today.'

'As I speak I'll try not to use any unfamiliar words. Although each year seems to bring us newly-coined words to memorise. Remember when we first heard of Yuppies – Young, Upwardly-mobile Professionals? And Dinkys – Dinky stood for Double Income, No Kids Yet. My wife says I'm more of a Nappy – Nackered, Ancient and Permanently Pickled. And to think when I married her I was a Willing, Able, Likely Looking Youth – that's right, a Wally.'

'Before we start, here's a question for you: do you know which uses more muscles, frowning or smiling? Frowning uses far more. True. That's probably why you folks are smiling at me – you're not happy, you're just lazy.'

'Your chairman has given me some valuable guidance on my speech this evening. I visited him in his office and on the wall behind his desk he has a painting of a man in a wig and gown with a large china potty on each foot. I said, "What do you call that?" and he said, "A judge in chambers. Would you like to buy it?" I said, "No, I like the judge but I don't like his pose." That's the last time I buy a jokebook in an Oxfam shop ....'

'Part of the fun of preparing a speech is looking in the dictionary and accidentally discovering uncommon words and meanings, like "millihelen". A millihelen is the amount of female beauty required to launch one ship. Ahah, an audience with a classical education! Here's one more definition before we start – charisma. Charisma is that special attraction that a fat, bald, ugly dull person with ten million pounds has.'

'Thank you. I stand before you on a date doubly significant in history. It was on this day in 1851 that the first message was sent by underwater telegraph ... it said, "Help, we're drowning."

'And on this same day in 1913 the first pair of trousers was sold with a zip instead of buttons. Before then the worst thing a man could get caught in was a lie.'

If you've spoken to the same group before
'I'd like to say thank you to those who've written very complimentary letters to me about my previous visit to your enjoyable function. Here's a typical example chosen at random: "Dear Bob Monkhouse, I've seen you in person

several times but you're still a mystery man to me. How do you spend your spare time? Where do you go in the evenings? What do you do with your money?" Hold on, this is from my wife.'

CLOSINGS

All purpose

'And by way of farewell, something P G Wodehouse observed: where one goes wrong when looking for the ideal partner in life is in making one's selection before walking the full-length of the counter.'

'And I'll close with a parting word of advice from Erma Bombeck. Never go to a doctor whose office plants have died.'

'And a final word of advice to women everywhere from the great Mae West: "Don't let a man put anything over on you except an umbrella."'

'Who was it said, "If drinking tea makes your eyes hurt, try taking the spoon out of the cup"? I don't know but it seems a good tip to end on.'

'And as I bid your farewell, here's a health tip: never tell a man using a chain saw that he has bad breath.'

'And try to remember the wise words of my lawyer – honesty is the best policy but insanity is a better defence.'

'And in parting, consider the words of the writer, Josh Billings: "Love looks through a telescope; envy through a microscope."'

'And here's a closing thought from the American comedian Stephen Wright – everywhere's within walking distance if you've got the time.

And as a wise woman once observed, "The trouble with being punctual is that no-one is there to appreciate it." (*Check your watch*) But I'm sure you'll appreciate my punctuality in finishing dead on time.'

'In conclusion, thank you for your attention and your kind response to my words. It's like my mum used to tell me, "Cast your bread upon the waters, my son, but make sure the tide's coming in." And as a parting shot, this advice to women, "Never wear a long necklace while operating a blender with the top off."'

'It was the Canadian humourist Stephen Leacock who wrote, "A speaker should endeavour to conclude with an observation that combines humour with truth." Fortunately for me he also provided this example, and I quote: "There is only one beautiful child in the world – and every mother has it."'

'Here's a thought – any time you think you have influence, try ordering around someone else's dog.'

'I leave you with this wish: may you be in heaven five minutes before the Devil knows you're dead.'

Female audience

'So goodbye – and remember your mother's warning, girls: "That glance over cocktails that seems so sweet – may be less charming over shredded wheat."'

'Please, drive carefully, alcohol and petrol don't mix. Well, they do mix but they taste terrible.'

'Thank you for your kind attention, enjoy the rest of your evening and, in the words of the Northern Irish comedian Roy Walker, "May the path to hell grow green from the lack of your feet."'

'Let me leave you with this word of advice: if you have a jar with a lid that's stuck, here's the easiest way to get it open – put it on the table and tell the children to leave it alone.'

'So thank you and good evening, my friends, and I leave you with this depressing information: the secret of immortality dies with me.'

'And I leave you with what some bright lady said about cosmetic surgery. She said, "I don't have anything against face-lifts but I think a good rule of thumb is that it's time to stop when you look permanently frightened."'

'I leave you with a piece of advice from Erma Bombeck: "Never lend your car to anyone to whom you have given birth."'

'Here's a closing observation from the American comedian Red Skelton: "Any kid will run any errand for you if you ask at bedtime."'

'In the words of the song, "I wish you love." And to any wives here who feel unloved may I suggest that you try taking a greater interest in your husband's hobbies. Hire a detective.'

'Finally, a closing thought. You know something that occurred to me only recently? It's a shame that most parents weren't given their neighbours' children because those are the only ones they know how to raise.'

'You know, finding myself addressing an audience as nice as you makes me grateful for my good luck. Mind you, I'm also grateful for my bad luck. Without it, I could never explain my mistakes. Thanks to you, tonight hasn't been one of them ..... '

'A wise woman I know once remarked, "Marrying a man for his good looks is like buying a house for its paint." I hope you found my words less superficial than that.'

'You've no idea how it feels to come to the end of another brilliantly written and impeccably delivered speech. Unfortunately neither have I.'

'And let me leave you with the reminder that we don't live in a logical world. If we did, men would ride sidesaddle.'

'I'd like to stay longer but my wife/girlfriend is getting pregnant and I'd like to be there when it happens.'

'And I leave you with this piece of human nature: that it's easier for us to suffer in silence if we're positive someone is watching.'

'I'll leave you now with love and a quote from the immortal Mae West: "Love cures everything except poverty and toothache."'

'A wise person once said, "Never mind criticism. Most knocking is done by people who don't know how to ring the bell."'

More all-purpose
'Before I go, some advice from the entertainer Richard Stilgoe: "Don't listen to that man who's trying to sell you a chain of off-licences in Saudi Arabia – you could lose more than your money."'

'Today's parting advice? If you're feeling lonely put a "FOR SALE" sign in your front garden. It's surprising how much friendlier your neighbours get when they think you're moving.'

'It's all over for now but here's a bit of parting advice for husbands: men, try praising your wife. Even if it does frighten her at first.'

'I don't know who said this but isn't it true? Nothing makes a person more productive than the last minute.'

'After living as long as I have, a thought occurred to me: life is ten per cent what you make it and ninety per cent how you take it.'

'So that's all for now except for saying to anyone feeling blue, "Cheer up! We may be worse off than we were yesterday but we're better off than we will be tomorrow."'

'And in parting, I offer a comforting reminder in these times of apparent moral laxity: there are no new sins – the old ones just get more publicity.'

'Perhaps I've touched upon a few predictions that none of us can be sure of. Well, to conclude, here's something I'm quite sure of – things work out best for those who make the best of the way things work out.'

'That's it, I've told you all I know but then, as my old dad used to say, "You're never quite as stupid as when you think you know everything."'

'And, hey, if your ship hasn't come in, swim out to it!'

'A last piece of advice from my old grandmother. She used to say, "The only person you have to try to be better than – is you."'

'Here's my parting shot: you don't get ulcers from what you eat. You get ulcers from what's eating you.'

'The person who never steps on anyone else's toes is standing still. And if you want to make your dreams come true, stay awake.'

'I'm going to stop now because I only have three minutes left of my allotted time and I usually need that for my applause.'

'A final word of advice: there's a time and a place for everything. For instance, saying, "But enough about me, let's talk about you" is fine at a party. But in a Confession Box ....'

'As someone once said, "Do unto others as you would have them do unto you ... unless you're a masochist."'

'And I bid you farewell with words to heed: tell your boss what you really think of him and the truth shall set you free.'

'And in closing, may I quote the last words of my cousin Gavin: "If at first you don't succeed ... so much for bungee jumping."'

'Let's never forget that everything's relative. There's this man, ninety-eight years old with a weak heart, and he broke a mirror. Now he's overjoyed that he's going to have seven years' bad luck.'

'Remember, if you get gloomy just take an hour off to sit and think how much better this world is than hell. Of course, it won't cheer you up much if you expect to go there.'

'As someone once observed, "The thing that leads most people into debt is trying to keep up with the people already there."'

'I'd like to close on a piece of useful advice but it's in short supply these days. I read in the paper the other day that if your shoes smell bad you should fill them with kitty litter and that'll absorb the odour and your shoes will smell fine. Sure, unless, of course, you have a cat. Duh!'

'Friends, if you can smile when everything around you is going wrong ... then you've probably figured out who to blame it on.'

'And finally, a suggestion to any new parents who may be here today: if you have any advice to pass on to your children give it to them while they're still young enough to believe that you know what you're talking about.'

'In conclusion, as my grandpa used to say, "Idle hands are the devil's workshop – or a slow day at the massage parlour." He drank a lot, did grandpa.'

'I'll close with a question from the deadpan comedian Jack Dee. Why do parents always take their children to supermarkets to smack them?'

'Until we meet again, let's never forget the wisdom of astrologer Russell Grant when he consulted his prune stones at breakfast and decided not to tinker with his tailor but to soldier on until he met a sailor.' (*The Two Ronnies*)

'I'll leave you with the words of May V. Smith who said, "The only place you find success before work is in the dictionary."'

'Who was it said, "If pigs could fly, Scotland Yard would be the third London airport"?' (*Warning: that line can give offence to some.*)

'And here's an eternal truth: no matter what you do, someone always knew you would.'

'Who was it said, "If you can smile when everything around you is going wrong – you're probably a repairman"?'

'And I'll leave you with a new proverb: a closed mouth gathers no feet.'

'Just a wee thought to end on: the most important things in life aren't things.'

'The Chicago talk show host Oprah Winfrey said this: "Lots of people want to ride with you in the limo, but what you want is someone who will take the bus with you when the limo breaks down."'

'Bye for now and remember: those who can't laugh at themselves leave the job to others.'

'The American journalist Linda Ellerbee made a nice observation for us to end on. "I want to know," she said, "why, if men rule the world, they don't stop wearing neckties."'

'Today I leave you with the words of my maternal grandmother: "One thing you learn by watching the clock is that it passes the time by keeping its hands busy."'

'An American writer named Kay Ingram said this: "The straight and narrow path would be a lot wider if more people used it."'

'A parting thought: married men have two ages. When they want to remain faithful but don't, and when they want to be unfaithful but can't.'

'And I leave you with this simple fact of life: you know your children are growing up when they stop asking you where they came from and refuse to tell you where they're going.'

'Henry Ford, the founder of the Ford Motor Co., said it: "When everything seems to be going against you, remember that the airplane takes off against the wind, not with it."'

'The American author Mark Twain said it: "If you tell the truth you don't have to remember what you said."'

'Has this ever struck you? That it's more than a coincidence that the person who is feeling no pain is also insufferable.'

'I'll leave you with an opinion from the American comedian Rita Rudner. She thinks men who have a pierced ear are better prepared for marriage. They've experienced pain and bought jewellery.'

'I leave you with advice from the American film star Shirley MacLaine who says the best way to get husbands to do something you want them to do is to suggest that perhaps they're too old to do it.'

'To those of you going on holiday, I wish you bon voyage to Greece, Turkey Cyprus or whatever happy haven you've chosen. Personally, I'd like to know what's wrong with a good old-fashioned British holiday, a friendly pub, decent pint of ale, a game of darts, a bit of a laugh and a good ruck with the locals after closing time. I don't know why more people don't go to the Costa Brava.'

'Let me leave you to ponder on the question of the day: could you kill a vegetarian vampire if you hammered him through the heart with a fillet steak?'

'And finally a conclusion from Dr. Billy Graham who said that truth isn't really stranger than fiction. We're just not as familiar with it.'

'I'll end with the words of the Rev. Sidney Smith: "Every time I want to criticise a woman I remember where God got his materials from."'

'As for me, I don't ask much of life, I just want to meet an attractive wife who's looking for a way to spite her husband.'

'Over (x) years making speeches have taught me one thing: he who laughs last is writing down the joke.'

'Let me end by assuring you all that yes, there is justice in this world. Yesterday the fella stealing my tyres was run over by the fella stealing my car.'

'One last tip for the ambitious teenagers: before you decide upon your aim in life, check your ammunition.'

'Someone said it: life is like a grindstone. Whether it grinds you down or polishes you up depends on what you're made of.'

'Just a closing thought – if you find a path with no obstacles it probably doesn't lead anywhere.'

'The speechwriter Mitch Murray said it: "In life the sky's the limit, so rise above the crowd. Perhaps you'll never be a star but you needn't be a cloud."'

'Here's something to consider: fear will make you hesitate. Hesitation will make your fear come true.'

'And I'll take my leave of you with my motto, Carpe Diem – seize the day. In her book *Values* Marva Collins wrote this: "Mr. Meant-To has a friend, his name is Didn't Do. Have you wandered down their road, Postponement Avenue? They live together in a house, it's name is Never-Win. And I'm told the house is haunted by the ghost of Might-Have-Been."'

'The American comedian Paula Poundstone says adults are always asking kids what they want to be when they grow up because they're looking for ideas for themselves.'

'Look for the good in everything because it's there to be discovered. The motivational speaker Zig Ziglar spoke the truth when he said, "Too many people find fault like there's a reward for it."'

'And to conclude – isn't it odd? We're all self-made but only the rich will admit it.'

'This is National Dental Week and here are three tips from Ken Dodd that will help you to keep your teeth: see the dentist twice a year, brush after every meal and keep your nose out of other people's business.'

'The film director Frank Capra succeeded by following his instincts. He put it this way, "A hunch is creativity trying to tell you something." I've got a hunch he was right.'

'Someone said it before but it's worth repeating: experience is a great teacher – only trouble is, you get the tests before you learn the lessons.'

'Here's a wish I can't help wishing – I wish I were what I was when I wanted to be what I am now.'

'A final smile – an interviewer asked Victor Borge if he played any other musical instruments. "Well, yes," replied Borge. "I have another piano."'

My favourite after-dinner crackers

In April 1988 Martin Dunn, Assistant Editor on *The Sun*, phoned me after I had been presented with the After-Dinner Speaker of the Year Award by the President of the Guild of Professional Toastmasters, Ivor Spencer. The ceremony took place in the beautiful Belgravia reception rooms of Moet et Chandon Ltd, courtesy of Viscount Marchwood and his fellow directors, and naturally I was called upon to 'say a few words'.

'Send me your twenty best after-dinner lines,' he said. 'There'll be a cheque for £1,000 sent to the Stars Organisation for Spastics if I get them by tomorrow afternoon.'

He got them first thing in the morning. In fact, I sent him thirty of my smartest all-purpose speech gags so he could pick out the twenty that suited *Sun* readers best. I figured he could omit the ten subtle ones.

I would like to have sent him some great lines I've heard from other speakers over the years but he was after my stuff. Pity. I could have included a marvellous line from a speech made for the Food and Drink Federation by Donald Thompson, MP, Parliamentary Secretary to the Ministry of Agriculture. Donald rose to propose the Toast to the Federation, surveyed the Great Room of the Grosvenor House Hotel with interest and said:

'This is the first time I've spoken in this room ... except during other people's speeches.'

I could have mentioned the introduction to a rival wit by Kenneth Williams:

'Our next speaker is one you'll remember for the rest of your life. If you have a phenomenal memory. And absolutely nothing else to think about. And you meet with a fatal accident on your way home.'

Or this introduction from the Texan comedy writer Joe Hickman who squinted at the page in his hand and said:

'It's my privilege and pleasure to introduce a public speaker of the highest magnitude, a man whose wit is legendary, who is sought after by every organisation, who honours us by his presence here tonight ... and who writes his own introductions.'

Or the opening George Burns used when he rose to address the famous Friars Club in New York. His lifelong friend Jack Benny was also being honoured that evening and had lost the toss to decide which of them should speak first.

'I want to thank the Friars for giving Jack and myself this beautiful dinner and it's a good thing you didn't wait much longer. At our age, every time we sit down to eat it could be the Last Supper.'

And he ended a typically great Burns speech by saying:

'In conclusion I want to thank the Friars for honouring me tonight. But before I sit down I must tell you I thought of a very, very funny closing line. It's hilarious – but I just found out that Jack Benny thought of the same line. And since, as I've said, we've been friends for fifty-five years and to show you what a nice man I am, I'm going to let Jack do that line and I'm going to sit down without getting a laugh.'

When a function was held in a particularly shabby hotel, it was the *Carry On* films scriptwriter Talbot Rothwell who said:

'Far be it from me to criticise my accommodation but you know there's something lacking in a hotel when you notice that the Gideon Bibles are in paperback.'

In reply to some jocular ribbing from a rather aggressive Advertising Director, I recall hearing a Production Manager respond:

'Contrary to popular belief, Fred's mother and father were married. Not to each other, no, but they *were* married.'

US President Ronald Reagan was always a master of comic delivery, knowing the value of self-deprecation. He told a mainly Hollywood audience:

'When I say something, people know I'm not lying – I was never that good an actor.'

Campaigning for election Reagan reminded his listeners that the Roman emperor Diocletian had tried price controls and they hadn't worked. Then he added, 'And I'm the only one here old enough to remember that.'

It was airline chief Freddie Laker who kidded his staff:

'If you have any further ideas about how to rescue this company, please drop them in the suggestion box down the hall. And don't forget to flush it.'

So much for quoting others, now I'll quote me. Bearing in mind all that has been said about the correct placement of comedy in a speech and the suitability of the comic dart to the perfect bullseye, here are the thirty crackers I 'sold' to *The Sun*. Apply them shrewdly to the right occasion and the right people and you'll score.

1. Mr. Chairman, I really enjoyed your little talk. It was up to your usual substandard.
2. Thank you for that speech. Linguists tell us there are 35,000 useless words in the English language and you hit every damn one of them tonight.
3. And so we come to the speeches. The speeches give everyone who didn't get indigestion from the meal a second chance.
4. Preparing for a speech is like preparing for a big football match. You eat correctly, get plenty of rest and abstain from sex. And I promise you that I have eaten correctly, have had plenty of rest, and will abstain from sex during this speech. (Immediately afterwards, watch out!)
5. We all know the boss is a strict man. He once received a ransom note for his children and sent it back to the kidnappers for re-typing.
6. But in your defence, Sir, we know that we haven't seen all your management skills and techniques. Company policy expressly forbids beatings.
7. Aggressive? This morning, the receptionist said, "Have a nice day," and he said, "Don't tell me what to do!"
8. What a fine dinner tonight! And everybody's trying to lose weight, I even know a cannibal who's on a diet – he only eats midgets.
9. You know what we can all expect tomorrow, don't you? A Champagne Hangover: the wrath of grapes!
10. The Company Secretary doesn't like to drink – it's just something to do while he gets drunk.
11. Our Advertising Director can take credit for a lot of things, but he's always willing to share a little with the person who actually did it.
12. What can I say about our Sales Director? He's been called cold, rude, self-centred, arrogant and egotistical. But that's just his family's opinion.
13. Our Marketing Manager is a man with a conscience. He's not an ordinary drunk. He donated his body to science and he's preserving it in alcohol until they use it.
14. Let me salute our Financial Director, a man so mean, he found a box of corn plasters, so he went out and bought a pair of tight shoes.
15. George is spruced up for this occasion. Even went to the barber. After the new barber gave him a really close shave, he asked for a glass of water. "Are you feeling faint?" asked the barber. George said, "No, I just wanted to see if my face is leaking."
16. Among us tonight are politicians and doctors. Doctors are like politicians: they view with alarm so they can point with pride.
17. We have some younger folk present and I admire the youth of today. I saw

these kids carrying a sign: "MAKE LOVE NOT WAR!" I'm married – I do both.

18. I greet the insurance experts here tonight. They know that there are two kinds of liars in car accidents. Both drivers.

19. The ladies look lovely but they don't know everything. Ask any woman her age and nine times out of ten she'll guess wrong.

20. Take Joan Collins. She even lies about her dog's age.

21. Maybe it's true that *life* begins at forty. But everything else starts to wear out, fall out or spread out.

22. Don't worry about avoiding temptations as you grow older. They will avoid you first.

23. Today we're having a retail sales boom. It's weird to go shopping! You would never believe how many different things a bargain hunter would rather have than money.

24. And how about today's morals? The big question is: Can a girl be a good girl if she returns home from a date with a Gideon Bible under her arm?

25. I just hired a detective to watch my wife – not that she's unfaithful. I just want to know where she is when I am.

26. Is my shirt behaving? I always have trouble with laundries. The last one I sent my shirts to lost the buttonholes.

27. We have legal experts here tonight and I respect you all. My lawyer helped me lose eight stone of fat – he got me a divorce.

28. We have medical experts and I respect you too. My doctor's very shrewd. He kept me in his waiting room so long I caught four other diseases.

29. Two chaps talking at a bar. One said, "I got married because I was tired of going to the launderette, eating junk food and wearing socks with holes in them." The other fellow said, "That's funny: I got divorced for the same reasons."

30. Finally, a toast to your sex lives: "May you live as long as you want to … and want to as long as you live."

You asked for it

In the years during which this manual has circulated I've had a number of requests from readers. In this section I'll try to deal with two of the main ones: what to do with hecklers and how to enhance your negotiating skills.

TACKLING THE HECKLING

The professional comedian is accustomed to squelching the occasional heckler and often uses standard lines that he's memorised:
'Why don't you sit next to the wall? That's plastered as well.'
'Sorry but the rule here is "the one who's nearest the microphone speaks" – but keep shouting so the bouncers will know where to find you.'
'You've got a point there, pal – but wear a hat and no one'll notice it.'

They're fairly harsh put-downs and suit a cabaret club setting. But for the corporate or social speaker something softer is usually required.
Two rules to observe:
1. *Keep your reaction to interruptions light-hearted and agreeable.*
2. *Don't hit a heckler with a hard insult until he's annoyed the audience enough for them to want you to do it.*
Here's how I prefer to deal with a loudmouth at first: whatever's been shouted and whether or not you've heard it clearly, pretend you haven't.
'Sorry, I didn't quite catch that. What did you say?'
He may go quiet on you:
'Not worth repeating, eh?'
Or he may say it again: 'Very good. But I don't think the people on the far side of the room heard you. Could you shout it out again for them?'
By this time he looks rather silly and you don't. If he repeats his line for the benefit of back of the room, shake your head regretfully and say, 'Nope, it didn't get a laugh that time either. See if you think of something funnier for us later on.'
If he subsides, you can use a throwaway line 'God bless you, sir, and may

He come for you soon' before continuing your speech. If he doesn't subside, give him enough room to hang himself.

Once a heckler has become an irritation to the crowd, the gloves can come off. I've scored off many a barracking drunk with spontaneous responses, some of which are listed below. If you employ them, remember these are gaglines and may not be as effective without an extemporised feel about them. So do try to give them a freshly invented air. If you know the heckler and what he does for the company or society, you have a great advantage. Use a sweet delivery; it's twice as potent as a rough one.

'You must excuse Jim, ladies and gentlemen. He's always given this firm an honest day's work. Sometimes it took him a week to do it ....'

'Don't mind our Jim. He pioneered the idea of staggering working hours, you know. Usually the first two after lunch.'

'Jim's having an identity problem. People know who he is.'

'Thank you, Jim. You have all the creativity of the office photocopier.'

'Ah, Jim, I'll say this for you, you've got class. All of it third.'

'You know, Jim, there are some things in life that go without saying. Be one of them.'

"Would you please cover one of your ears? You're creating a draught.'

That dynamic duo Hale and Pace gave a demonstration of the art of instant mutual abuse on ITV with exchanges like,

'You are an investigating forefinger. You get right up my nose!'
'You've got so much cheek you could be Roseanne's arse.'
'You're a mating cow, you're so full of bull!'
'You're Monica Lewinsky in a pair of slacks – all mouth and trousers.'
'But, hey, mate – Pope's knob, eh? No hard feelings.'

It takes the cheek and personality of such a popular pair to get away with raunchy lines like those but, if the crowd is young and up for a bit of real impudence and rude fun, go for it.

'Give him a chance. For him it's a night out. For his family it's a night off.'

'Feel free to express yourself – by Red Star perhaps.'

'Oh, so dinner isn't quite over. We have an extra portion of pickled tongue.'

'I need you like Van Gogh needed stereo.'

'Now here's a suggestion for you: why don't you clip battery leads to your nipples and jump-start your brain?'

'Yet another argument in favour of abortion – retroactive!'

'I didn't know there was a full moon tonight.'

'There you have living proof of the theory: the smaller the pip, the bigger the squeak.'

'As Mary said to Joseph, who needs you?'

Or, if you really want to dish it out, these two have a real shock effect:

'Half a million sperm and yours had to win!'

and

'Oh please! If I want to listen to an arsehole, I'll fart.'

PERSUASION AND PERSEVERANCE

When you recall the best speeches you've ever heard, from Winston Spencer Churchill's 'I have nothing to offer but blood, toil, tears and sweat' to Martin Luther King's 'I have a dream,' you have superb examples of the art of persuasion.

When you address an audience, persuasion is your purpose. Your objective must be to inspire and reassure those who already agree with and appreciate you and to convert those who don't.

Step by step you are entering into a negotiation: first, by establishing your credibility. The audience's trust and confidence must be won. As you fight your corner, you must be seen to be honest and fair.

We all negotiate every day of our lives. We deal with children, customers, friends, bosses, employees, salespeople; every time you want something from somebody or somebody wants something from you, there's a degree of negotiation involved. Since I've been the Chairman of several successful businesses and charities, it's been suggested that I share my experience.

It's that ability to bargain well that helps you to succeed in life, whether in little matters or those of real importance. It's a series of deals; if you'll do this, I'll do that. What's paramount is how you get what you want without creating hostility or resentment, the skill you use in reaching a mutually acceptable result. And that's the very same give-and-take persuasion that's required in a speech intended to win votes, raise charity funds or put over your point of view convincingly. So how is a negotiation best prepared ?

Keep Your Eye and Mind on the Target

Never lose sight of the outcome you most desire. Before you meet any opposition you should give thorough consideration to what you're ready to surrender to achieve your most essential goals. Think through every possible scenario, the best case you'll strive for, the worst case you'll settle for. Don't go into any negotiation without having as much information as you can possibly get and setting out your optional strategies should you meet a brick wall. You don't want to give up or storm out, your cause may be lost, so always have other ways to conduct the discussion. A wrestler varies his holds according to his opponent's counter-moves, just as a crack salesman can change his approach to introduce an alternative way of completing a transaction.

Let Air and Space into the Exchange

An old Chinese proverb says that if one word does not succeed, ten thousand are of no avail. I think that depends on how nimbly your argument is conducted. To be merely persistent in repetition of your position is counter-productive and makes you appear intractable. But if you can relax your stance enough to allow in the oxygen of free and decent conversation, to explore your two positions and your feelings about them, sweet reason can breathe more easily. Deadlocks are eased by discussion. Tell each other about your various difficulties and worries. The more you promote the expression of your opposition's concerns, the greater your right to set out your own and expect equal understanding.

Winning a Deal Often Comes From Perseverance

So long as both parties can negotiate with integrity and fair play, your proposals and the counterproposals they produce should be sensible at least.

On this basis, keep trying to improve the deal with your end in mind but remain pleasantly steadfast. Don't be afraid of conflict, that's part of the game, but try to envisage conflict as a positive force for improvement, especially for you.

If you lose sight of what you really need to achieve, you'll fumble the ball. Keep to a middle course between the stubborn and the conciliatory. Make too many concessions, give in to weariness and hardheaded opposition, and you'll wind up with a bad conclusion. Pile on excessive pressure, refuse to budge on minor issues and play the hard man, and you may have to quit empty-handed. Therefore take the middle course between these extremes and persevere. I've attended so many meetings where lengthy arguments that had sometimes appeared impossible to resolve were suddenly settled when the less persevering of the two parties said, 'Look, this is getting to be too much bother over a small difference. If you feel that strongly about it, okay.'

It's Not Personal

When an audience is unresponsive, it's foolish for the entertainer to take it personally. It's a professional encounter, not a romantic date. The same goes for negotiating. Rejection of your point of view or your proposals isn't an insult to you. Keep your ego out of it. For the performer, it's the performance that's on offer, not the person who offers it. A dismissal of your case isn't an attack on your self-esteem. You have to defend your strategic position without taking its repudiation as a slap in the face. Likewise, don't take up an attitude likely to offend the sensibilities of the people you're dealing with. It's a trap that wise negotiators avoid. See the other fellow's point of view and ask him to see yours. Once again, it's fairness and honesty that can make progress in negotiating while making sure that personal vanity doesn't get in the way.

Listen and Learn

Hear what the man opposing you is really saying. Winkle out his actual thinking, give genuine attention to his needs. Show that you take him seriously and have regard for the aspects of the deal that worry him. Then you can express your own honest thoughts in turn.

You hold differing positions but chances are you also have concordant interests and shared aspirations. Talks need not break down while both parties remain conscious of mutually beneficial results.

Share those positive elements. Marriages have been saved by applying these simple principles.

And ask him what lies behind some of his demands. If you learn how his reasoning works, you have a chance to find a new way of coping with it.

In this way you may detect a flaw in his attitude, an obstinacy that isn't based on a real condition but only upon his reluctance to lose face. That's when you can save his pride by turning what he sees as a loss of his prestige into a gesture of magnanimity on his part – simply a matter of words. By altering his perception of a weakness into a strength you are saluting his ability to compromise as wise and generous.

Don't Reveal Your Bottom Line

You have entered this negotiation with an ideal conclusion in mind. That's your secret. Although your opponent may have a rough idea what you're aiming for it's unlikely that he's aware of your detailed thinking about how you hope to wrap things up. Keep your final resolution under your hat until everything has been laid out and discussed fully. Why? Two good reasons. One: because bluntly stating your intentions makes you appear disinterested in reasonable argument. And two: because immediately giving the game away robs you of the chance to examine the entire picture and the possibility of discovering ways to improve your deal and make a better closure than you'd hoped for.

Spreading out all the options on the table as they affect the interests of both parties helps you to concentrate on how you want things to work out in days to come. Never mind the useless baggage of yesterday. Tomorrow is where you want your negotiation to pay off.

There's a third reason for not letting slip your dream solution: it's a discourtesy. It reveals a mind-set that won't allow for the other person's real needs. If you feel resentment, disdain or even hatred, talk yourself out of it. Emotion clouds intelligent reasoning.

It's self-defeating. Before any negotiation you should check your approach for any trace of B.A. – Bad Attitude.

You may not like the person you have to talk to but remember, it's important to keep personalities completely separate from the problem. You can enter the arena as enemies, strangers or close friends and still come out the same way having successfully negotiated an okay deal for yourself.

Don't stick to fiddly little points because you've made up your mind to do so before the meeting began. Compromise isn't a bad thing when it produces a satisfactory result. You can safely give way to a point of principle while never surrendering to pressure.

Are You Persuading From a Principled Point of View?

If the eventual outcome you want is fairminded, it cannot be withstood except by the bloody-minded. Like any good defence lawyer, when you truly believe in the justice of your case you can argue it with conviction. Honesty is your ally, not only in putting forward your views but in recognising that everyone's interests must be served.

Oh, yes, you can run into trickery, untruths, bribes, psychological warfare and dirty tactics of all kinds. When you do, the same rule applies: honesty is your best policy. Get it out in the open. Let it be known that you're aware of the duplicity and suggest getting back onto a basis of fair play. This can often disarm a trickster without the necessity of calling in an arbitrator.

Now that I've had my say about negotiating techniques, let's see how some of it applies to public speaking.

Persuasion is what they have in common. Preparation is what they both require. Before facing Prime Minister's Question Time in the House of Commons, Tony Blair has been quoted as saying, 'Know your stuff and know your enemy.'

The negotiator may have to cope with blind hostility and, of course, that's far less likely for an orator. Nevertheless it's vital to know in advance if your audience has a group attitude to any subject you intend to cover.

Like the negotiator, think through how you want and expect the audience to react to your speech. Imagine their thoughts, what they'll find acceptable, what they might not agree with and how to sell your point of view.

Win the audience's trust and, as in any well-argued transaction, you and they will both benefit.

Guidelines for a memorial service

Since the first version of this book was published I've had to speak more and more often at gatherings paying tribute to an old friend or colleague who has died. It's one of the problems of getting old. People you've known throughout your life start to drop off the twig and you find yourself at the cemetery more often every year.

Americans almost always deliver eulogies at burial or memorial services, while we in Britain tend not to be quite so effusive about the dear departed. Nevertheless, the word 'eulogy' is derived from the ancient word for praise and it's considered proper to stress the nobler aspects of the deceased's nature rather than speak ill of the dead.

Most memorial services are a bit of a trial. Everyone looks stressed out, including you if you have to speak. But try to remember that everybody knows how difficult your task is and allow that sympathetic understanding to calm any trepidation you may be feeling.

When George Gershwin died, the novelist John O'Hara wrote, 'They tell me Gershwin's dead but I don't have to believe it if I don't want to.'

I love that quote and I used it twice, at the cremations of two beloved friends. You may find it helpful too in expressing the feeling that dear ones are never truly gone while they live on in the hearts and thoughts of those who loved them.

Bear in mind that the feelings of affection and respect you'll be trying to convey are shared by all present. You can speak in the simplest terms with no fear of criticism. If your words come from your heart they will form the truest tribute to the person whose life you are celebrating.

On deeply sad occasions that seem to allow no room for levity, you may wish to take your source material from the greatest authors. Try looking in the shop where this book was bought. Collections of quotations can supply many profound thoughts from brilliant minds who have considered the tragedy of loss. They have found ways of saying things that uplift the spirit in the midst of sorrow.

Victor Hugo spent half a century writing prose and verse, history, philosophy, drama, romance, tradition, satire, ode and song but here's how his great soul found utterance as old age came upon him. Perhaps the words he wrote then will find an echo in the hearts of those assembled.

'You say the soul is nothing but the result of bodily powers. Why, then, is my soul more luminous when my bodily powers begin to fail? Winter is on my head but eternal spring is in my heart. The nearer I approach the end the plainer I hear around me the immortal symphonies of the worlds that invite me. It is marvellous yet simple. It is a fairy tale and it is history. I have tried to do all I could and yet I feel I have not yet achieved the thousandth part of what is in me. When I go to my grave I can say like many others, "I have finished my day's work." But I cannot say, "I have finished my life." My day's work will begin again the next morning. The tomb is not a blind alley; it is a thoroughfare. It closes on the twilight, it opens on the dawn.'

That passage just happens to be a favourite of mine but literature is full of beautiful and soothing phrases for those afflicted with grief. These expressions can come to your aid when you're called upon to 'just say a few words' about a person for whose life you want to give thanks.

I always believe in stating the reasons for your presence at any function and a memorial service is certainly an occasion to set out your purpose.

'We're here to give thanks for the life of John Jones, a man who inspired so many positive qualities in everyone present – loyalty, trust, good humour and gratitude for every day allotted to us. And let's not allow our sorrow to overwhelm that feeling of thankfulness that we have been privileged to know and love our dear friend. We are all poorer for his loss but so much richer for his having touched our lives.'

Keep your homage to the subject upbeat. Don't emphasise the tragic aspects or speak at length upon his illness or suffering – grief can be sincerely recognised and accepted but there's no need to dwell upon anything negative.

Focus instead upon everything good and praiseworthy about the person and share your happiest memories of him. Mention how kind or patient or generous he may have been to his friends and family. If he enjoyed successes, include them in your description of his life.

I've always found humour based upon truthful recollection to be a great asset. Maybe you can summon up a funny incident that shows the person in a favourably human light or even tell his favourite anecdote.

When the person has died young these elements in your address are even more essential. Avoid stressing the injustice of a life ended so early or the wretchedness of the cause. Speak of the importance of his life to everyone who knew him and how much he'll always mean to you, living on in fondest memories.

A short Bible reading or even a final prayer may seem appropriate if the service is a religious one.

And, please, don't feel apologetic or embarrassed if you are overcome with emotion while speaking. Everyone will feel that emotion with you. Take your time to pause, collect yourself and continue when ready.

That shrewd American comedian and philosopher Will Rogers is one of my heroes. He once said, 'When I die my epitaph is going to read "I never met a man I didn't like". I'm so proud of that I can hardly wait to die so it can be carved. And when you come around to my grave you'll probably find me sitting there proudly reading it.'

I used that quotation at the service given for an old pal who combined the very same qualities that Will was revealing about himself – a real liking for people and a degree of forgivable vanity about it.

Lastly, please don't allow the sombre nature of a funeral to affect your clarity. There are people at the back who need to hear what you're saying.

I've attended so many funerals and memorial services where those paying verbal tribute think it's necessary to lower their voices and speak reverentially.

Once again, you've got a message to deliver. Put it over. Don't yell, of course. We don't want to wake the dead, do we?

Making it motivational

Another field of public speaking that has expanded since the first publication of this manual is that of the inspirational and motivational exemplars.

Though not called upon to deliver such material myself, I have had the opportunity of watching some very influential speakers driving out scepticism and stirring up feelings of enthusiasm in their corporate audiences.

Some have had the advantage of famous achievements to justify their right to speak – two were heroes, one in the Falklands and the other in Desert Storm, another was a brave woman who had fought and won through a well-publicised battle with cancer. Others have adopted the use of props, slide shows and magic tricks to put their message across and, correctly handled, these can be very effective in holding group attention and illustrating a point memorably.

But without your having a conjuror's skills or being a stage cartoonist, juggler or balloon twister, you can still make a strong motivational pitch with the use of seven simple articles – a very big glass jar, a scoop, a flask of coloured water and four containers or bags with stuff in them.

Have these items on a small table to one side and have another larger table in front of you. A radio mike would be useful for this demonstration but, if haven't one available, be sure your handmike doesn't get in the way of your actions. The flask should be concealed in the fourth bag.

After opening your address, tell the audience, 'I wonder how many pieces of coal would fill that glass jar?'

Reach into the first of your bags and pick out a apple-sized lump.

'What would you say? Five, ten, fifteen?' Wait for guesses. 'Let's see, shall we?'

Carefully take the pieces of coal from the bag and place them inside the jar, counting loudly as you go until no more will fit inside.'How many pieces was that? And would you say the jar is full?'

As soon as they've agreed, open the second container or bag and lift out a handful of coarse gravel, letting it flow back into the bag to show its rough consistency.

Raise a scoop. 'I wonder how many scoops of gravel would really fill it up? Any guesses?'

Steadily lift scoopsful of gravel out of the bag and let them flow in between the lumps of coal in the glass jar. When no more will go in, ask the spectators, 'Now would you say the jar is full?' Someone will probably be thinking ahead and will say, 'Not really, no.'

'Good!' Dip into your third bag and lift out a handful of fine sand. Again, let it flow back into the bag to demonstrate its fluid nature before you begin to pour the sand into the jar, filling up the remaining tiny spaces between the coal and the gravel. Shake the jar to help the sand to settle, smile at the people and ask, 'Now you say the jar is full?'

A bright bunch will suspect you of tricking them again and will answer, 'No.'

'Wonderful, you catch on quick!'

Out of the fourth bag you produce your flask of coloured water which you pour into the jar full of coal, gravel and sand till it reaches the brim.

'Ladies and gentlemen, would you agree that the jar is at last full?' They should respond with impatient yesses – there may even be a few voices raised to demand to know what you think you're proving.

Take your time. 'Does anyone here know the point of all this?'

Some suggestions may be made, not all complimentary. Or some cleverdick may pipe up with, 'Efficiency. There always room fo fit more work into a given space or time period.'

You might compliment anyone who offers a good guess.

'But you haven't quite seen the point of this simple demonstration. What I'm trying to show you is this. If you don't put the coal in first, you'd never ever get it in. I could have used apples or stones or lemons or tennis balls, the result would be the same. The big stuff has to come first. And that's true of every phase of your life – personal and professional. Put the main ingredients of your life in first, the coal – then the smaller things, the gravel – then the sand and finally the water.

'Plan your progress so that the great things take pride of place, like your spouse, children, parents, brothers and sisters, love, health, home, job, money – they should all go in as your first priority.

'Now you can add the next thing in order of importance, the gravel. And that represents your holidays, hobbies, social life, sport, music, luxuries and so forth. With all those in place, you can add the little things that make up the sand and the water of your life, the non-essentials. But never let them come ahead of the great things of your life. The coal must come first!

'It's so obvious now, isn't it? Consider the people you know who never put the big considerations ahead of the rest. I know a man, a man I like, who has just screwed up a major project because he took his eyes off the main objectives and got bogged down by side issues and minutiae. You could say his failure to organise was putting the sand and gravel in first, leaving it too late for those symbolic chunks of coal.

'Think of this demonstration in any terms you like, it's a lesson that will apply to everything you attempt. Writing a speech? Get the coal in first.

Making a sales pitch to a client? Get the coal in first.

'Don't be diverted by lesser matters, self-indulgences, confusions, jealousies, vanity, petty rivalry, minor details – they're all sand and water and mustn't get in the way of what you're really trying to achieve.

'Fill up your life the right way. Organise your thinking. Do what Arthur Scargill failed to do for the miners – get the coal in first!'

If you decide to make this demonstration, choose your items with care. Pieces of coal should be the right size and shape without a tendency to flake or crumble and they must be carefully washed and even lacquered for smooth handling. Of course, you needn't use lumps of coal if you'd rather handle something else. I've already mentioned fruit and tennis balls and stones but you could try pieces of granite, glass Christmas tree baubles, seaside pebbles or golf balls. This would require some changes in your verbal presentation and there may be an unfortunate whiff of sexism in exhorting a mixed audience to 'Get your balls in first!'

Your validity on video

After more than fifty years in front of TV cameras I've gained my share of tips for avoiding traps.

And now that video is so widely used at conferences and in other corporate presentations, you should also be aware of these.

Autocue Eyes

Good TV presenters and directors know how best to measure the distance that separates the performers from their autocues over the camera lens. Too far away may test your eyesight to the point where your expression will appear strained. Too close and your eyes will be seen to move from left to right as you deliver each line, making you appear to be reading rather than addressing your viewers directly. Yes, of course you *are* reading but, if it's apparent, it's also off-putting and inclined to draw attention away from your message. Also, sideways eye movement looks shifty.

Your script on the screen should be about six or seven feet away so that you can see the entire page displayed without having to squint or swivel your eyes ro read it. An experienced video team may advise you of this but then again, if they're busy with other worries or scared of you, maybe not.

Make-up

Many men hate wearing make-up but videotape sees you differently from the naked eye. The camera exaggerates flaws, darkens a five-o'clock shadow, picks up glossy sweat and reddens patches of skin. A first-class make-up artist can make you look more like yourself, cleverly emphasising your more attractive features and minimising imperfections. If it's worth your while to appear on video, it's worth your while to look as good as you can.

Distracting Clothes

However smart and expensive your clothes may be, they have to be quiet enough not to drown out your words.

DRESS SUBTLY

In a Bournemouth summer season I made my first stage entrance in a dazzling silk suit with white polka dots on a solid blue background. My opening routine scored laughs but not the guffaws I was hoping for. After a week or so my fancy suit was accidentally stained and, while it was drycleaned, I made do with a plain tan suit from my private wardrobe. Suddenly my gags were getting the big roars I'd hoped for.

The answer was immediately obvious and I'm sure you've guessed it. Part of the audience's attention had been unconsciously diverted by the eye-catching spotted suit. The same rules apply for you on TV. Nothing too exciting. If you're wearing a blue jacket, choose a pale blue shirt or blouse and don't wear a tie that would put a female flamingo in heat. Choose your least noticeable scarf, necktie or cravat. You don't want your outfit to be a bigger subject of attention than your message.

Broadly striped clothes are out. The horizontal ones make you look stocky; vertical are okay but they should be narrow so as not to resemble a deckchair.

Fine patterns should be checked with the cameraman because many a handsome herringbone or dogstooth cloth has strobed on TV, giving the disconcerting effect of crawling and fluttering. You'd do better to select solid colours and gentle shades with no design in particular.

Just as long as they won't ask if your outfitter is Stevie Wonder.

How Long Are the Long Shots?

Check whether or not your feet will be in vision at any point. If so, you'll want a shine on your shoes and the kind of socks thay don't sag to reveal a seductive glimpse of hairy leg. Women who kick their shoes off when working should avoid the habit on video.

The Mike's Fine But Where's the Battery Pack Going?

If your voice is being picked up by a handheld boom or a desk mike, this doesn't apply. More often than not however, the sound engineer on your video will want you to wear a radio microphone on your tie, lapel or blouse. That's okay if you're seated throughout your presentation; the wire can go under your clothing and the battery pack somewhere behind you on the chair. But if you're standing or walking, he'll ask you to wear the pack. It's not big, about the size of a packet of cigarettes, but it's heavy enough to weigh down your pocket in a way your tailor didn't anticipate. That's when the sound man will want to tie a small cloth bag on a black ribbon round your waist and have you carry the battery under the back of your coat.

For years I had my suits measured and made to make me appear as well turned out as possible on TV. Then the sound guys would fix my mike's battery pack to the back of my trousers, adding enough to my girth to pull a buttoned jacket completely out of shape. I eventually caught on and had a wooden block made which I wore in the small of my back while being measured for a new suit. The most obvious solution is to leave your jacket unbuttoned. Either that or insist that the battery pack is strapped to your ankle. I know it can be done because I've done it.

And in the case of a frock made of delicate material, don't let some horny-handed technician clamp the microphone's clip on you. Ask him where he wants it to be and then fix it there yourself; too often the wire has snagged on something and done its version of bodice ripping.

The Jewellery Problem

If you're at a desk, rings can rattle against wood. Video lighting tends to reflect distractingly off metal tie clips, brass buttons, enamel badges, diamonds, lapel pins and jewellery of all kinds. You should remove or conceal such ornamentation for the camera.

When I'm on TV I only ever wear a simple gold ring and that's only because it has great sentimental value for me. I got it from grandfather when he was on his deathbed. And I must say, for an old fellow who was dying, he put up a hell of a fight.

In and out of humorous classics

Doctor Sigmund Freud says there's no such thing as a new joke. No, nor a new plot, a new tune, a new design or a new day. Everything new is derivative to a certain extent, Siggy, I understand that. But I've spent the past forty five years or so making up jokes by shuffling familiar words and ideas into a novel order. In the course of this rather absurd but lucrative career, millions of sentences have been produced which, when spoken out loud, make people laugh. These could reasonably be regarded as new jokes because no one has thought of them or said them before. But after they've been heard, then what are they?

Well, the weak ones are scrap paper. The moderately funny ones go into the file for twisting, polishing and possible further employment. And the really good ones become old friends. There is nothing wrong with using an old joke. On the contrary, if it's funny and appropriate, there is everything right with using it. You just need to grace it with the proper setting.

Once you have got a few well-chosen yarns in your repertoire and they've gone down well a few times, there's no need to abandon them for the sake of change. Provided the audience is different, you can find security in repeating stories in which you have confidence in all sorts of contrasting situations. Just ease your way into them with words that seem to apply only to the particular place, time and people.

The old friend is a reliable laugh-getter that both you and most other people can still enjoy. You may have heard a comedian tell a comic tale that's immediately familiar to you and thought, 'I like this story.' Then you've heard the happy laughter from his audience and perhaps you've wondered how much of it was surprise and how much recognition, pleasant recognition of an old friend. For the speaker, such old friends are just as trustworthy – but you've got to treat them well and introduce them properly.

The dear old BBC provides the right language for this sort of thing. Old radio shows aren't old, they're 'listeners' requests from the Golden Age of Broadcasting.' The umpteenth showing of some TV warhorse isn't a repeat, it's 'another chance to see the vintage Award-winner.' Re-runs at Christmas and Easter are 'traditional fare' and if the star died last week it's a 'special tribute'. Our old friend only needs the same treatment – introduce it as 'a classic'.

With one word – 'classic' – you simultaneously disarm critics and set a seal of semi-immortality on the yarn you're about to spin. You're not claiming it's new. On the contrary, you're proclaiming its status as a Golden Oldie. No-one can jeer at the age of an antique, can they?

The way a speaker flows naturally from his speech into an anecdote takes a little thought, but it's so worthwhile in its effect. How often have you winced at a clumsy transition or a hoary cliché: 'Which reminds me of the story of ....'

I heard a speaker interrupt himself in just this way with a quite unsuitable joke and it's stayed in my mind ever since. Here was this physicist giving us some simple and enthralling stuff about the miniature universe of the atom, when he decided we needed a laugh. His narrative switched as if he'd changed TV channels and he was off into a story about a teacher lecturing on sex morality. The punchline got a titter because it was, and still is, a good little joke. And then he jerked us back into his sub-atomic world so fast we all suffered tiny hernias in our attention. Wrong story for the moment, wrong way in and out of it.

Use the examples below to suit circumstances which are appropriate to you, your speech, the setting and the audience. If you plan to keep a card-file, put these in for starters. The format is, I hope, self-explanatory. I have suggested an 'In', followed by a suitable story, followed in most instances by an 'Out' which sets you back on course for the rest of your speech. Where there is no 'Out', I have assumed you can safely be left to carry on by yourself.

FOLLOWING A BRILLIANT INTRODUCTION 'For that magnificent introduction, I thank you … I think. It was so good, I can hardly wait to hear what I'm going to say. I just hope I can live up to it.

'These are what are known as "mixed feelings", a term once defined as watching your mother-in-law drive over a cliff in your new car. There's another classic example that comes to mind but this one is true. Shortly after the death of Noel Coward, Peter Ustinov was preparing a BBC TV programme in tribute to his memory and his music. A rather arrogant young composer buttonholed Ustinov with an elegy he had composed in honour of Coward and he insisted on playing it to him at once. Tolerantly Ustinov postponed his next appointment and listened to the twenty-minute piece until the last note had died away. "Well?" demanded the composer. "What do you think?" "I think,"

said Ustinov, "that it would have been better if you had died and Noel Coward had written the elegy."

'Dear Sir, I think it might have been better if you were making this speech and I had made the introduction .... '

THIS BEAUTIFUL CITY 'Your city is blessed with its magnificent cathedral, historic churches, many fine libraries and parks and a widely envied museum. The museum staff are especially helpful to ignorant visitors like me.

'I asked an attendant, "How old is that Roman pottery?" and he said, "Seventeen hundred years, five weeks and two days." I said, "How can you pinpoint its date with such astonishing accuracy?" And he said, "No problem, sir. It was seventeen hundred years old when I took this job and I've been here exactly five weeks and two days."

'But my inquiries about this function have provided much more reliable information ....'

THE USE OF LANGUAGE 'Some people use language to express thought, some to conceal thought. Far too many of us use it to replace thought. Mark Twain had his own views on languages. He said that a gifted person ought to learn English in thirty hours, French in thirty days and German in thirty years. But is the English tongue really so simple?

'Only last week I noticed an odd quirk in our language. When we talk about an East Wind or a West Wind, we mean the direction the wind's coming from. But when we say clockwise or anti-clockwise, we mean the direction the clock's going to. And that, I suppose, explains why we run out of wind before we run out of time.

'If I'm not careful, I may be in danger of doing the opposite – running of time before I run out of wind ....'

BEING CLEARLY UNDERSTOOD 'Naturally, we all want to be understood. Equally naturally and important, none of us wants to be misunderstood. To that end, we should employ language not only to express our ideas but also to convey them comprehensibly to others.

'The IBM scientists could have been working for years now on the perfect translator, a computer which could turn the United Nations Building from a Tower of Babel into Harmony Hall. Their acid test of an ideal machine is that when it has translated a phrase from the first language to the second, it should be able to translate the same phrase from the second language back to the first and come up with the exact original wording. A laudable ambition but one which doesn't account for our English ambiguities. Into the computer went *our well-known saying, "Out of sight, out of mind". It was translated into Russian. Then the Russian version was retranslated to English again. Guess what! "Out of sight, out of mind" came back as "Invisible insanity".*

'Doesn't that accidental phrase describe to a T the workings of certain political minds?'

TOUGH PROBLEMS, SIMPLE SOLUTIONS 'Even the most experienced panel of experts can miss the answer to a professional dilemma precisely because they are experienced. They are able to identify all the complex difficulties obstructing their normal procedure – but a fresh and unpractised eye may be more alert to the existence of another approach altogether.

'*Remember the classic tale of the lorry that got stuck under a bridge and a crowd gathers and no-one knows what to do? Some say tear the top off the lorry, others say dismantle the bridge. The argument rages – top off the lorry, dismantle the bridge. Finally a small child at the back asks, "Why don't you let the air out of the tyres?"*

'We should always be open to a new approach to our problems from someone with an uncluttered viewpoint. They may let the air out of our tyres before an opponent takes the wind out of our sails ....'

AGE AND ADVANTAGES 'As one grows older, Nature compensates a little bit for one's diminishing powers in curious ways. Some old folk increase in their philosophical understanding and feeling for human nature.

'*My great-uncle's a wonderful octogenarian living in an Old Folk's Home. There's a little old lady in there who's got her eye on him, and she claims to have gypsy blood. She told me, "I feel so close to your great-uncle. Why, I can even tell where he's from and how old he is." I said, "How?" and she slid her hand under his bedsheet, groped about a bit and said, "You're a Capricorn, still very vigorous, married three times, 81 years old and born in Penge!" She said. "You're right! How can you tell all that?" She said, "You told me yesterday."*

'Growing old isn't so bad when you consider the alternative ....'

CUSTOMS AND MOTIVES 'When first encountering any human mystery or arcane custom, look first for the simplest motive. People have acted according to the same basic reasoning since history began.

'*I was travelling in the Atlas Mountains of Morocco, a part of the world steeped in tradition and superstition, when I saw an Arab riding a donkey while his wife walked fifteen paces behind him. I said, "Excuse me, but why are you riding the donkey while your wife is walking?" and he said, "She hasn't got a donkey." A few weeks later I was in the Lebanon and I saw another Arab riding a donkey while his wife walked fifteen paces in front of him. Again, I asked why and he said, "Landmines."*

'Obviously, Women's Lib has yet to make its mark in the Middle East, whereas here tonight the ladies have it firmly established ....'

PROSPECTS AND RESPONSIBILITY 'Are we ready to accept the responsibilities of future success? Well, whenever I'm asked if I can handle a situation, I tend to examine the thinking behind the question.

'Unlike the Irish suitor courting the lovely O'Hannigan girl. Old Man O'Hannigan interviews the lad. "Do you think you're earning enough to support a family?" says he. "I certainly do," says the boy. "Think carefully now," says O'Hannigan. "There's twelve of us."

'But we face challenges more cautiously examined and found to be acceptable ....'

IS THE CUSTOMER ALWAYS RIGHT? 'Keeping the customer satisfied is sound company credo. Can it be carried too far? Has a company ever gone bankrupt by allowing its customers to dictate the style of service, variety of product or its trading policy? Well, the line has to be drawn somewhere this side of running a charity.

'The Chief Executive of Italy's biggest supermarket chain told me a story about a rather unimaginative thief who plans to rob one of their suburban stores. He needs an excuse to go up into the manager's office so he thinks, "I'll complain about the choice of goods." He walks in and there's the manager on his knees putting the day's takings in the safe. "I want to complain." "Yes, sir, what's your complaint?" "You've got no coffins." "Coffins? In a supermarket? Are you mad? Go to the funeral parlour. We don't sell coffins!" The manager turns away to close the safe and the thief seizes his chance, pulls out a cosh and cracks him over the head – THWACK! And the manager says, "Okay, okay! I'll get some in tomorrow!"

'Italy also gave us the Latin motto which is implicit in all customer-related trading – Caveat emptor, let the buyer beware. I would add let the vendor beware too. When you cut back on your prices, you may have to cut back on your quality and so eventually on the number of customers. A bargain takes two and both should benefit ....'

REFUSING AN INVITATION 'In accepting your invitation to attend this function, I expressed my gratitude. Had I been unable to accept, I should have expressed my regret. But when we decline an invitation just because we don't want to go, how hypocritically sorry should we pretend to be?'

'*George Bernard Shaw was in no two minds about it. An aristocrat seeking his acquaintance sent him an invitation: "Lady Proctor will be at home on Tuesday, August the Tenth, between four and six in the afternoon." Shaw returned the invitation. Underneath he had written: "Mr. George Bernard Shaw likewise."*

'All very well for GBS, but I believe the cause of diplomacy would suffer without its kindly little lies. Shaw, on the other hand, could never resist giving an honest retort if it had the force of wit.

'*The self-admiring dancer Isadora Duncan sent him a passionate invitation to father her next child. "Think what a child it would be," she said, "with my beauty and your brain." Shaw replied at once. "Madam, think what a child it would be if it had your brain and my beauty."*

'Had I both the brains and the beauty, then, I might have been one of those rare and privileged creatures whom Shaw would invite to the opening nights of his plays. And here was the biter bit.

'*Shaw's new play,* The Apple Cart, *opened in 1929. To Winston Churchill he sent an invitation with the words, "I enclose two tickets so that you may bring a friend – if you have one." Churchill returned the tickets with this reply. "Regret a previous engagement, but could I have tickets for the second night – if there is one?"*

'Speaking for myself, I am more than content to give this single performance. Two nights of this speech and I might have no friends ....'

SPECTATOR SPORT 'For those who can't enjoy taking part in physical sports for whatever reason, BBC TV has proved to be a great boon. But while they began by bringing us football, cricket and tennis, lately they seem to think that we are a nation of snooker addicts.

'*I read the other day that the keepers at Regent's Park Zoo have even altered feeding times to fit around transmissions from the Sheffield Crucible. What's more they say that many of the animals like to watch it as well. At night the snake creeps into the elephant's enclosure and says, "Fancy a frame?" The elephant says, "But we've got no tables, balls or cues." The snake says, "Well, let's see which one of us can do the cleverest tricks and we'll award the points just like they do in snooker." The snake curls himself into a hoop and rolls all the way around the elephant: "That's worth a red and a yellow – three points!" The snake forms a spiral and corkscrews through a bale of hay: "A red and a black." The elephant tap-dances: "Another red and a black. How are we going to decide a winner?" The snake says, "I can win this easily. I'll go right up your trunk, straight through your body and out the other end!" The elephant says,*

"If you can do that, you'll be the winner all right." So the snake shoots right up the elephant's trunk, wiggles through his body and he's just about to make his exit when the elephant sticks his trunk up his other end and says, "How's that for a snooker?"

'I can't see Steve Davis doing better than that. But in every situation, there's more than one way to snooker your opposition ....'

NB: If the image of Jumbo's trunk in his rear end is too picturesque for your audience, have the elephant cross his back legs.

FALLIBILITY 'We should never be deceived that an individual's achievement of high office and great influence means that all that person's private weaknesses have been conquered, although the responsibility of power often means that personal fallibility must be concealed to preserve the unflawed image expected of a leader.

'Men who served in the Royal Navy under Admiral Sir James Lawry Gregory called him "Pope Gregory" because he was never wrong. Throughout the Second World War, while maintaining rigorous RN discipline and doing everything by the book, he was the hero of the North Sea convoys and led brilliant naval exploits in the Mediterranean. It seemed the man had no weaknesses at all, except for one curious little idiosyncracy. Every morning

after breakfast he would retire to his state room, open his strong box and study a piece of paper. For years, every man who served under him speculated about what was on that page. Then one day the great admiral was called to the Bridge urgently and left his quarters without locking his safe. While he was busily occupied, two of his junior officers dared to slip into his cabin and look at the note that he read every morning. It said, "STARBOARD ON THE RIGHT, PORT ON THE LEFT".

'If human greatness weren't founded upon a little weakness, it would be neither so great nor so human ....'

ACHIEVING A RESULT 'Persuading someone to do what you want them to do can often run you right up against a flat rejection. We'll never get anywhere battering our heads against that sort of brick wall. It's much wiser to pause and consider how to climb over it, walk round it or loosen the mortar bit by bit. There's nearly always another way to get people to react as you wish them to.

'*Ask that legendary farmer in (name of local town/village) whose livestock was upset by the motorists speeding past his property at eighty mph. His solicitor told him it would take time and money to bring his case to the attention of the Council and argue for a suitable police notice to be erected at the roadside, and even that would probably be ineffective. The shrewd old farmer came up with his own sign and it says, "PLEASE PROCEED WITH CARE. NUDIST CAMP CROSSING AHEAD."*

'I shall approach the subject of what I hope to persuade you to do with equal caution ....'

OBITUARIES 'One way to get your name in the newspapers is to walk across (name of local busy street) reading one. I think it was Brendan Behan, the Irish playwright, who said there's no such thing as bad publicity unless it's an obituary notice. And it was another great Irishman, the comedian Jimmy O'Dea, who marvelled over the obituaries in the press. "Isn't it wonderful," he said, "how many people manage to die in alphabetical order?"

'*Here's my favourite obituary ever, clipped from an old issue of the (name of local paper). "FLINDERS, Frederick John: Accidentally killed last Saturday when a bullet ricocheted while he was endeavouring to shoot a rabbit in his vegetable garden. Surviving are his wife, three children and one rabbit."*

'It makes you ponder on what you'd like them to say about you ....'

THE CENTRE OF INTEREST 'An audience's attention can move away from a speaker for the oddest reasons. The Sales Director may have the boardroom in his spell when the tealady trundles in and zip, he's lost his grip. A phone rings, a waiter drops a tray, someone topples a glass of wine, or, worse than these, everyone in the room keeps glancing at the Chief Executive after every pleasantry to see if he thinks it's funny before they dare laugh. Comedians suffer that same problem when Royalty is present and very visibly so. The famous owner of London's Stork Club, Al Burnett, once admitted he always sent his musicians offstage while he did his nightly patter routines because their glum faces cast a gloom over the crowd.

'Even his Holiness Pope John Paul II is not exempt from these vagaries in group interest. He was Archbishop and Metropolitan of Cracow when he was created cardinal in 1967. As such he attended many glamorous functions where beautiful and shapely ladies were the natural centre of attention. But the 47-year-old cardinal confessed to a friend and diplomat, "The snag with these grand affairs is that every time a lovely lady is presented to me and curtsies in a low-cut gown, no-one is looking at the lady. Everyone is looking at me to see if I'm looking at the lady."

'Of course, I have you gentlemen at a disadvantage right now. While you're looking at me, I'm looking at the ladies ....'

BIOGRAPHY 'Your Chairman asked me to supply a biography and I was happy to oblige. I was just grateful he hadn't asked for a pedigree.

'A social climber I know in (name of local town) has just lost interest in his family tree. He paid a genealogist four hundred pounds to dig up information about his ancestors. Now he's had to give him another hundred quid to keep him quiet.

'Why pay money to have your family tree traced? Just go into politics and your opponents will do it for you ....'

FIRST IMPRESSIONS 'For every salesman, creating that first impression is crucial. You start by winning the customer's confidencce, right? But what comes next? Even the least perceptive customer knows that appearances can be deceptive.

'Unlike the gullible missionary wandering in the African jungle when he comes face to face with a hungry lion. Too late to run, so the missionary sinks to his knees and starts to pray. To his amazement the lion also goes down on his knees and starts to pray. The missionary cries, "It's a miracle! A moment ago I had given up all hope and now this savage beast joins me in holy prayer!" "Quiet", growls the lion. "I'm saying grace."

'This is one deal the missionary doesn't want to close. But how should you go about winning over the customer?'

PERSPECTIVE 'It's always wise to spare a moment to see the other person's point of view. From their angle, matters may seem entirely different.

'*A family of lions, sprawled out under a clump of trees in the Safari Park at Longleat, looked up as a car packed with eight staring tourists drove slowly past. And the father lion remarked to his brood, "Dear oh dear! It's really cruel, the way they keep them caged up like that."*'

RETRACTIONS 'If I've done anything I'm sorry for, I am always willing to be forgiven. And I'll always accept an apology if it matches the size of the damage.

'*I remember when Norman Tebbit was the subject of an insulting article in Robert Maxell's* Daily Mirror. *A week later he ran into Maxwell in the gentleman's toilet at the Savoy Hotel. As Maxwell washed his hands he said, "You know, Norman, I've been thinking about that article we ran last week and I've decided that it was totally unfair. I apologise." And Tebbit said, "I accept your apology, Robert – but next time, why don't you insult me in the gent's and apologise in the paper?"*'

WORTH, NOT COST 'It's not the price of a thing that's important, it's the value ... as in the case of an inexpensive but strategically placed button.

'Charlie Chaplin was already a multi-millionaire on a day in the early Thirties when he was visiting the studio of his friend Pablo Picasso. But Chaplin was raised in the poverty of London's East End and the lessons of childhood never left him. Picasso made a sudden gesture and accidentally spilt some paint on Chaplin's white slacks. He said, "I'm so sorry, Charles! I'll get some spirit and remove it." And Chaplin said, "Please don't! Just leave the paint where it is and sign my trousers."'

'As Thoreau said, "All good things are cheap, all bad things are dear."'

HIRING AS REQUIRED 'I've heard it argued that a resident expert on the payroll will cost less than engaging him as a freelance for each individual project. From his point of view, that might seem quite fair – the security of a regular salary compared with separate fees which subsidise idle periods. But it doesn't take into account the psychology of the maverick, stifled by such security and at his best in precarious independence.

'A tramp came up to me in (name of local town), obviously an educated man down on his luck. He said, "Excuse me, sir, I don't like to beg but could you spare me a few pounds?" I said, "Yes, but will you spend it on food, drink or shelter?" He said, "No, sir, to be frank I shall spend it on the favours of a lady of the night, a pleasure I haven't had for months." I said, "If you want a woman, why don't you get married?" And he said, "What, and have to beg for it every night?"

'A man who doesn't care what people think can generally be found at the top of the ladder or at the bottom ....'

COMMUNICATION AND COMPREHENSION 'No-one enjoys the time wasted trying to decipher the gobbledegook of civil service forms, legal documents, even the instructions for programming a video. But are we never guilty of sending messages couched in terms familiar to ourselves but totally impenetrable to the recipients?

'True story: in 1923 a pregnant woman ran into the Aberdeen telegraph office and told the operator that her husband had gone off to London to have a banner made for the Church of Scotland Christmas Bazaar & Pageant, but she had forgotten to tell him how large the banner should be, or which hymnal words should form the inscription. So she sent her husband the following telegram: "ANDREW McALLAN, ST PANCRAS HOTEL, LONDON. DEAR ANDREW, UNTO US A SON IS BORN, TWO FEET WIDE AND EIGHT FEET LONG." Andrew never returned to Aberdeen.

'Customers sometimes never return if the messages they get from us are mysteriously or thoughtlessly expressed ....'

CRITICISM 'Few of us really enjoy criticism but we can usually appreciate its value to us if it is both constructive and fair. Unfair comment or plain abuse is unacceptable – although it can be very entertaining to those who aren't involved.

'Our local Amateur Dramatic Group got a bit ambitious this year and staged their version of King Lear. It attracted quite a lot of comment but I think this criticism should give you a pretty good idea of what it was like. It's from our local paper: "On (date), the (name of local town) Players performed Shakespeare's King Lear to a full house. The only real benefit to be derived from this production is that it can at last clear up the question as to whether this play was written by Shakespeare or Bacon. All that has to be done is to open up both their graves and see which one turned over last Friday night."

'Please, if you have anything as wittily cruel to say about my performance, let it remain as secret as the grave ....'

HONESTY 'We must be astute in our honesty. Too many people think that those qualities are mutually incompatible, that honesty precludes craftiness. It just isn't so. You can be one hundred per cent honest and still use your wits.

'I heard of a lady in (name of local town) who lost her handbag. Some honest bloke ran after her and returned it. She said, "That's funny – when I lost it there was a twenty-pound note in it. Now there are four five-pound notes." And the chap said, "Yeah. The last time I found a lady's handbag, she didn't have any change for a reward."'

TECHNOLOGY 'Technology is filling our offices and homes with appliances smarter than we are. And some of us may be awe-struck by the computer whizzkids and their complicated apparatus. But we should never forget that the greater the invention, the simpler the common sense that created it.

'Whenever the great inventor Thomas Edison guided visitors around the displays of novel gadgets that filled his home, someone would always be sure to ask, "With everything here so modern and innovative, why do your visitors still have to push their way in through that old-fashioned turnstile?" And Edison would chuckle with delight and say, "Because, my friend, every single soul who forces his way through that old turnstile pumps three gallons of water up from my well and into my water tank."'

PIONEERING 'In every business the veteran loves to boast to the tyro how tough it was in the early days.

'Best bit of bragging I ever heard was a grizzled old plumber trying to convince his apprentice how hard the job was when he was learning to do it. He said, "You've got it soft, lad. In the old days they used to let us lay two lengths of piping. Then they'd turn on the water and we had to keep ahead of it!"'

THE LESSONS OF EXPERIENCE 'Experience is a great teacher. Only trouble is, you get the tests before you learn the lessons.

'I know a brilliant young chiropractor who was called in urgently to a London hotel to attend to a highly placed Emir from the Middle East. The Arab aristocrat was in agony until my friend's phenomenal skills at soothing angry vertebrae brought relief. After a week of daily treatment, the Emir was fully restored. The young chiropractor had no idea what fee to charge. He spoke to the Emir's London legal advisor: "What should I do? Treat him free as an honoured visitor, or would that be insulting? Should I ask him for one thousand pounds, or is that taking advantage of his wealth?" The Emir's legal advisor said, "Try this – submit your account but leave the amount blank. Simply write across the top of your bill the words 'THE EMIR IS ALWAYS FAIR'." Within a month the chiropractor received a cheque from the Emirate's Exchequer for twenty-five thousand pounds! He phoned the lawyer at once to tell him the good news and thank him. Next day the young man received an invoice from the lawyer for his services. The amount had been left blank and across the top of the bill were the words "THE CHIROPRACTOR IS ALWAYS FAIR".

'Not too painful a way to learn a lesson about taking professional advice. Perhaps it's time for me to offer some of mine – at no further cost ....'

HEAD HUNTING 'In every business talent is at a premium. The input of new and gifted recruits can revitalise flagging enthusiasm in factory, office and boardroom. Of course, when you go searching for talent, it all depends what you're looking for.

'I heard of an American basketball coach whose favourite fantasy is that a gorgeous, wealthy college student lures him to her dormitory ... where he meets her brother who is seven foot six.'

MEETING A DEADLINE 'I once had a boss who liked to give me jobs with precise deadlines and then let me know that he'd given the same task and the same deadline to another of his young aspirants for promotion. He reckoned there was no better spur than setting up a neck-and-neck race between his employees. And it's hard to deny that having the competition breathing down your neck can make you move faster than you ever dreamed you could.

'As in the classic case of the commuter newly moved to the countryside. Desperate to catch his train he called to a farmer busy herding his cows along the road, "Hey, grandpa! Is it all right with you if I take a shortcut across your field? I've got to catch the 8.15!" And the farmer said, "Go ahead, young fella – but if my bull sees you, you'll catch the 7.45."

'Next time you feel a deadline is beyond your reach, try to imagine that bull is closing in behind you. You'll reach it ....'

UNTRAINED ASSISTANTS 'There are many blessings to becoming an expert but one of the curses that comes with that status is the responsibility for training your apprentices. An assistant who is no assistance at all can be a distinct liability. Should it be part of your job? How else can your experience be passed on?

'The couple next door to me recently had to go to town on business so they

told their ten-year-old son to take care of his little sister. He said, "I'll take her fishing with me, she'll learn something." When his parents got home his face was dark. "Never again," he told his mother, "I didn't catch a single fish." She said, "Never mind, I'm sure she'll learn to be quiet next time." And the ten-year-old said, "It wasn't the noise, mum. She ate the bait."

'When your help is no help, hang on to this thought: there are many times when you can't get help, but there's never a time when you can't give it ....'

THE CARROT OR THE STICK 'These days we no longer expect to be nagged and badgered at work. Instead of being reminded of what failure will bring, we're encouraged by the rewards of success. Domestically though, it doesn't seem to have changed as much. According to a recent survey, 33 per cent of British husbands are henpecked. Do you know how they found out about that? Simple, they just asked the wives for permission to interview the husbands.

'It brings to mind the incredibly henpecked husband who finally did something without his wife's okay – he dropped dead. She was devastated. No-one to moan at, to harass and torment. Her neighbour was sympathetic. She said, "I can tell you're missing poor Claude." The widow wiped away a tear and said, "Oh yes. It seems only yesterday he came up the path, opened that front door, and stood there, letting two flies in."

'We all know which works better for us – the threat or the promise.

'Remember the king's head torturer who did horrible things to his prisoner to make him admit his guilt in a conspiracy, all without result. Finally, the king tried another tactic. And sure enough, the prisoner confessed. The torturer was astonished. He said, "Your Majesty, what new agony did you apply?" "None," said the king, "I just offered him something he wanted more than anything in the world." "What?" asked the torturer, and the king said, "To change places with you."

'It's been said before but it's still true – human beings will never work as hard for rewards as they will for greater ones ....'

WRONG CONCLUSIONS 'At a function I attended a long-winded speaker had been on his feet for forty slow minutes. Then he took a deep breath and embarked on yet another subject, the dangers of hastily formed opinions. He said, "When I look at your faces I make a judgement about how to speak. I am sure you would not wish me to jump to a conclusion." A voice from the back rang out, "Jump to it, run to it, but for pity's sake, get to it soon!" It's all too easy for any speaker to reach a conclusion – both the conclusion of his speech and wrong conclusion about its reception.

'When the Trade Union Leader Vic Feather had spoken at some length to a Workers' Co-operative in Shanghai, he sat down to total silence. No-one clapped, no-one cheered, no-one even smiled. Then a Chinese official rose and spoke for about the same duration in Cantonese. This time the audience broke into prolonged cheering. In a generous mood of resignation Vic started to join in the enthusiastic applause. An official from the British Consul caught his arm and murmered, "Not quite the done thing, sir – it's your speech they're cheering."

'I hope you won't feel that I need an interpreter to explain my choice of words to you tonight ....'

REGIONAL SENSIBILITIES 'It's easy to become so immersed in our own affairs that we begin to believe that all the world thinks and moves as we do.

'In Scotland they tell the classic story of a high-powered London solicitor who required a deposition from a farming family in Strathbogie. He phoned the opposing solicitor in Inverness and said, "I'll fly up there next Friday, talk to these farmers and spend the rest of the weekend along Loch Ness." The old Scots lawyer said, "Friday next? Oh, no, I don't advise you to come to this part of the world asking questions on Friday next. You would not get much of a welcome." The Londoner said, "Welcome? How would they welcome a summons from the judge?" "Och," said the Scot, "that would really put their backs up. You see, up here they're mindful of the fact that next weekend is Easter ... and the last time a person was ordered to be interrogated on a Good Friday, they crucified him."

'I too must be aware of certain sensibilities here tonight ....'

CO-OPERATION AND HOSPITALITY 'I thank the organisers for their kind co-operation and my hosts for their hospitality.

'I know a farmer from the Black Country who once explained to me the difference between the two. He said, "When two cows stand with their heads to each other's tails, flicking the flies off one another's faces, that's cow-operation. And when the same thing happens in the stables, that's horse-pitality."

'Ah, you're like my father who couldn't stand puns. He said he was contra-puntal ....'

VANITY 'I often think that when success turns a man's head it's a shame it doesn't wring his neck at the same time. But the overblown balloon is all the easier to burst.

'When the American star Harry Richman played the Leeds Empire in 1938

he boasted to the manager, "I'm so popular in New York, they're going to name a new cigar after me." The blunt Yorkshireman said, "Oh, aye? Well, I hope it draws better than you do."

'Nevertheless, when praise is due it must be given ....'

POTENTIAL CAPABILITY 'Computers, specialised electronics and high-tech systems apart – the truly unlimited capacity for our success lies in only one piece of apparatus, the human brain in the human body.

'They still tell the classic story in County Limerick of a great broth of a boy brought before the Regional Magistrate for the possession of a still. He denied using it to make illicit booze. The Magistrate said, "Come now, Sean, you can't expect me to believe that you haven't been making poteen. Why, the very fact that you own the necessary equipment is proof of your guilt." Sean said, "Then, by God, your Honour, you'd better charge me with sexual assault as well – for though I've never done it, I sure as hell own the necessary equipment!"

'Your future potential depends upon your quality, skill and determination – and, looking around me, I can see you sure as hell own the necessary equipment ....'

RESEARCH BEFORE JUDGEMENT 'Naturally I've sought some guidance before taking up your time here today. I checked my facts.

'Even judges seek information from their peers so they can do a better job on the bench. Monica, an elderly lady of the night, stood before the newly appointed Judge Marlowe. She appealed for leniency so pathetically that he had qualms about pronouncing sentence. He called a brief adjournment, then went to the chambers of a senior judge and said, "Harry, what would you give a sixty-year-old prostitute?" And Harry said, "About ten quid."

'When I asked your Chairman how much he would give a thirty-nine-year-old speaker, he said, "About twenty minutes."'

NB: Adjust the age to suit yourself.

RULES AND REGULATIONS 'Regulations are meant to do just that – regulate. On the other hand, rules are laid down to help us, not to rule us. Applied over-zealously they can begin to exist purely for their own sake and that's when they cease to help and start to hinder.

'As in the classic case of the rural West Country couple who decided to celebrate their son's fourth birthday by getting married. They rode their pony and cart into Truro and presented themselves to the proper official. He sent them off to get a licence. When they returned with it, he questioned the

bridegroom's name. He said, "You've put Joe – is your given name Joseph?" *"Yes, sir." "Then go back and fill it in correctly." Back they came with a corrected form whereupon he questioned the bride's name: "This says Beth – is your given name Elizabeth?" "Yes, sir." "Then go back and fill it in correctly." When at last they returned with every detail properly filled in, the Registrar scowled at the licence and said, "Well, I have no choice but to marry you but I want to make one thing perfectly clear. That son of yours will still be a technical bastard." And Joe said, "That ain't so bad, sir. That's what your clerk said you were."*

'I've been called a lot of things in my time but no-one ever said I was technical ....'

WORKING CONDITIONS 'A strong employer deserves a strong Union and vice-versa. If one of them is weak, both can suffer.

'Sir Philip Harris told me the classic story of one job applicant who said, "I like the job, sounds fine, but the last place I worked paid more, gave more overtime, more bonuses, subsidies, travel allowances, holidays with pay and generous pension schemes." Sir Philip said, "Why did you leave?" He said, "The firm went broke."

'That's the trouble with hard bargains – they can turn out to be hard on everybody ....'

THANKS TO EVENT CO-ORDINATOR 'This has been a marvel of organisation and for that we must give our unstinted thanks to the person(s) responsible for it.

'It's been as complicated a piece of administrative juggling as I've seen since my wedding day. I can still hear my bride-to-be saying to her mother, "Mummy, I've still got a million things to take care of and I do want everything to be as perfect as possible. I'm determined not to overlook even the most insignificant little detail." And her mother replying, "Don't worry, I'll make sure he's there."

'Well, tonight's organiser(s) made sure I was here too and I'm very grateful.'

SALUTING A CLEVER BUSINESSMAN 'Everyone allied in business has benefited from his acumen, either in terms of wealth or experience.

'I first learned to appreciate his application of sound business principles to every kind of occasion when I had the honour of attending his wedding. I remarked to his beautiful bride how I couldn't help but notice that all the guests were married couples. And she said, "Yes, that's my wonderful

husband's idea – isn't it clever? He said if we only invite married people all the presents will be clear profit."

'In my experience, just having his friendship over the years has been clear profit for me ....'

PATRIOTISM 'Intellectually I know that Britain is no better than any other country but emotionally I know it is. National pride has less to do with the State than with the state of mind. Of course, patriotism is a little out of style these days, although there are still some countries much admired for the nationalistic zeal of their people, and none more than Scotland.

'I once met a Scot from Wick in Caithness. As a lad he'd served hard to buy a bicycle and get a job as a delivery boy. With his savings from that he was able to afford the luxury of buying his old mother a train ticket to visit her sister in London, while he cycled down to keep her company. There she fell ill and, of course, a Scottish doctor was sent for. He told the lad that only the pure air of Northern Scotland could save his mother's life. Being a true Scot, he was equal to the occasion. He carted his bicycle up to his mother's bed, let the air out of the tyres – and she lived to be a hundred and two.'

'Well, that's what he told me. Maybe it was hot air all the time ....'

SARCASM 'Somebody once said that many a wife sends her husband to an early grave with a series of little digs. But sometimes sarcasm is the last resort of self-respect.

'As in the classic tale of the down-and-out scholar who pocketed his pride and made house-to-house calls in search of work. He knocked at the farmhouse door of the meanest old lady in (name of local town). She not only set him to work, she followed him about all day to make sure he wasn't idle for a moment. When at last mealtime came round, she grudgingly presented him with a slice of bread and butter and a large plate, in the middle of which was a very, very small spot of honey. Undefeated, the scholar looked up at her with polite interest and said, "I see, madam, that you keep a bee."

'That's the kind of thing I usually think of later and wish I'd said. A speech is too often the kind of thing you think of earlier and wish you hadn't said ....'

MERGER OR TAKEOVER 'Harmony needs two voices. There's always a common gain in what scientists call "symbiosis", defined in my dictionary as a "mutually beneficial partnership". What plain folk call "fair give-and-take on both sides".

'A widower friend of mine was sixty-five this year. Jim's still a handsome bloke, grey-haired but fit, and never one to say much until he has something *worth saying. Last week we were on the golf course when, after a silent hour or so of concentrated play, he said, "By the way, I'm getting married again." When he told me his fiancée's name I was a bit shocked. I said, "But, Jim, she's only twenty-four and you're sixty-five." He didn't answer. I said, "I must be honest with you, old friend. I don't believe in these May-December marriages." He still didn't answer. I said, "After all, December is going to find in May all the sweet glory and freshness of springtime. But, Jim, what is May going to find in December?" And Jim said, "Christmas."*

'To partners forming an alliance in trust and joint purpose, I can add little to that as a wish. Have a merry Christmas and a happy New Era ....'

DISPOSAL OF A LOSSMAKER 'Sentimental attachment has a sadly limited life in the competitive world.

'Like the classic little story of the desperate wife who tells her priest she wants a divorce. The good clergyman says, "Have you forgotten? When you married this man it was for life." She says, "I know, I know – but for the past eight years he hasn't shown any."

'Slimmer and fitter, we carry the signs of vitality and the prospect of a lively future ....'

PERSEVERANCE UNDER ATTACK 'A determination to stand fast in hostile circumstances is a quality that may at first be condemned as stubborn but which must, when steadily and goodnaturedly maintained, win respect.

'They still tell the story in the southern Welsh valleys of Michael Foot's first bid to become MP for Ebbw Vale. Whatever one's politics, there's no denying the wit and grit of young Mr. Foot as he fought to assume the mantle of his Welsh hero, the late Nye Bevan. Some of the diehard miners at the rally thought him too intellectual and too English. "Vote for you?" jeered one red-faced pitworker. "Why, I'd sooner vote for the Devil!" "Fair enough!" called out Michael Foot, "But in the event of your friend not standing, may I have your support?"

'Never give up the ship, or, as someone else once put it, "The opera's not over till the fat lady sings."'

SOFT ANSWERS 'Answering harsh criticism with instant protest may seem justified but it's often a knee-jerk reaction without regard to a desired result. Someone attacks you and your instinctive response may be angry, but will that bring you the conclusion you really want? Doesn't it pay to pause a moment to see if you can produce a more profitable response, a gentle answer that loses you nothing in terms of self-esteem.

'True story: The great photographer Karsh of Ottowa was dining at Le

Cirque in New York when Marlene Dietrich swept in. She had every eye upon her as she paused at Karsh's table, turned to him with disdain and proclaimed for all to hear, "Those photos you've just taken of me are atrocious! Hideous! You used to be the best but now you're pathetic. I remember the first pictures you ever did of me, they were fantastically beautiful." There was a stunned silence in the restaurant, during which everyone there heard Karsh say, "Yes, they were beautiful pictures, my dear, but you must bear in mind that I was twenty years younger then."

'Diplomacy need not be soft. And answering an insult with charm can produce a far more desirable effect ....'

PARTNERSHIP 'Sometimes one and one can add up to a lot more than two. Partners can inspire each other, even compete with each other, achieving far greater results as a team than either of them could do alone. But it's also important to understand the limitations of partnership.

'There's a vintage story the French tell around the Bourse. One partner says, "Our new secretary is such a sexy woman, in fact she makes love better than my wife." The next day his partner says, "You're right, she's sexy – and, mon Dieu, does she know how to make love! But not better than your wife."

'That's what I call putting the caring into sharing ....'

COURTESY 'There are many kinds of human behaviour which, although not essential to survival, make living pleasurable. Good humour, good fellowship, sympathy, patience, diplomacy and, perhaps, the one that is becoming the rarest of these, old-fashioned courtesy.

'Remember the man on the bus who stood up to give a woman his seat and she was so surprised she fainted. When she came round she said, "Thank you" and he fainted.

'I'm grateful that courtesy's not in short supply here tonight ....'

MAKING NEW FRIENDS 'Friendship can be based on long acquaintance or it can be instantaneous, forming itself quite involuntarily.

'She was standing, waiting for a bus, in a very tight skirt. And she had to wait quite a long time because, well, you don't find many buses in tight skirts, do you? She knew that when the bus came along she'd have trouble climbing aboard in her very tight skirt. So she reached stealthily behind her and loosened the zip. When the bus arrived, the man behind her in the queue picked her up and put her on it. She said, "How dare you do that!" And he said, "Well, after you opened my fly, I thought we were friends."

'From the warmth of your welcome, I think we are friends too ....'

FITTING IN WITH A NEW CROWD 'Some of us feel quite apprehensive about joining a new company and being accepted by new associates. It never turns out to be as difficult as we feared, except in the most abnormal circumstances.

'*Picture if you will a small garrison of British soldiers in a distant desert outpost. A new Army chaplain arrives and goes at once to report to the CO. "Good morning, Colonel, I'm the new chaplain." The colonel says, "Welcome to the regiment, you'll soon fit in, we have an excellent social life. Every Wednesday night all the lads get together in the mess, drink until they're sick as pigs and fall over, you'll love Wednesday nights." The chaplain says, "Actually, colonel, I don't approve of drinking." The CO says, "No matter, forget Wednesdays, you'll love Thursdays. That's the night we run our poker school." "No, sir, I never gamble." "Never mind, you'll enjoy Fridays. Every Friday night a bunch of the local native girls come over, ravishing women, all night long." "No, sir! I don't do that sort of thing!" "Good God, man, are you a poofter?" "Certainly not!" "Oh, then you won't enjoy Saturday nights either."*

'I did say abnormal circumstances. Ours are closer to normality ....'

GETTING TO KNOW YOU 'Now I never like to take a person at face value. Before I begin to deal with anybody new, I like to know something about their personal history, so that I'm not coping with an unknown quantity or quality.

'*Although I once made the mistake of playing darts for money with a stranger who told me he was new to the dartboard. I explained the rules and he proceeded to beat me hollow. I said, "I thought you told me you were new*

to darts?" He said, "No, new to the dartboard. I was a prisoner-of-war for three years and all we had was a set of darts. So I used to practise by pinning flies to the wall." I said, "But surely their blood made a bit of a mess," and he said, "Not if you pin 'em by one leg."

'On this occasion my spies have got me better prepared to meet you tonight.'

OVER-DEDICATION TO WORK 'When people are described as workaholics the term is seldom used pejoratively. We see hard work as admirable and so it is, but it can be overdone.

Sam, for example. Sam's a buyer, always on the road for a week at a time, buying, buying. In the course of his work he meets some attractive girls. One week his wife gets a telegram: "DEAR SADIE, CAN'T COME HOME, I'M STILL BUYING, LOVE – SAM." Five weeks in a row she gets that same telegram: "DEAR SADIE, CAN'T COME HOME, I'M STILL BUYING, LOVE – SAM" The sixth week she sends him a telegram: "DEAR SAM, BETTER COME HOME BECAUSE I'M SELLING WHAT YOU'RE BUYING."

'The rewards of hard work are many but overwork can turn them into penalties ....'

SELF-DISCLOSURE 'A speaker is always in danger of telling his audience more about himself than he means to. But isn't that true of all of us in our everyday encounters? Don't you find people reveal their true interests in what they say and how they say it without even realising it?

'I was in a saloon bar in (name of local town) when a priest walked in and said, "Can anyone direct me to St Broderick's Church?" And the barmaid said, "Your best way is to cross over by Our Price Records, turn right at the Next shop, left at Dirty Den's Disco and you can't miss it." The poor vicar didn't know what she was on about. Then the old soak next to me put down his seventh pint and said, "Listen, Rev, you want to go left out of here to the Red Lion, cross over to the Plough, pass the Coach and Horses and turn right at the King's Arms." Well, I just had to speak up. I said, "Father, the best route to take is left at the Pink Pussycat Massage parlour, right at the Naked City Striperama, past the Adult Book Shop, take the alley by the X Certificate Cinema and it's opposite Fanlight Fannie's Singles Club." And he said, "Thank God you were here, my son, or I'd never have found it."

'As you can tell, I'm not always on my guard about giving myself away – and on this occasion my defences are down again ....'

In and out of humorous classics

DISCOVERY 'Some men get discovered, others just get found out.

'*There's the classic case of the constable on night duty in the dead of winter who left his beat to run back to his house, chuck a pebble at his bedroom window until his wife looked out, and then call out, "Sorry to wake you, love, but I left my thick overcoat over the bedside chair. Throw it down to me, will you?" And she did and he put it on and felt much warmer. Then a bit later he nipped into the station for a cuppa and as he walked in, one of the lads said, "Blimey, George, how long have you been a Sergeant?"*

'Generally, though, worthwhile discoveries are not things that just turn up, they have to be turned up ....'

PERSONAL REASONS 'Often when we suspect people of having ulterior motives, what they really have are simply good reasons we haven't thought of.

'*Last week I asked my teenage son if I could borrow his record-player for the evening. He said, "Certainly, dad – do you fancy some rock and roll?" I said, "No, some peace and quiet."*

'I think I've an equally reasonable purpose for being here now ....'

'*Like the 60-year-old lady who went to the doctor for some birth-control pills. He said, "But why on earth do you think you need them?" She said, "A pill a day gets rid of my headache." He said, "But that's impossible." She said, "Listen to me – I live with my grand-daughter, a stunningly beautiful 16-year-old girl. Every morning we have breakfast together and, when she's not looking, I take one pill and pop it in her tea. Believe me, it gets rid of my headache."*

'Perhaps you'll allow me to share a headache cure with you ....'

AWKWARD SITUATIONS 'In your/my position, it's necessary to develop a skill at handling difficult relationships.

'*Like British Airways cabin staff. I recall a gorgeous stewardess who had two over-amorous men on the same flight to New York, both pestering her for a date, begging her for her address, phone number, everything. One even went so far as to pull his New York apartment key out of his pocket, jot down his address and beg her to "Please come and see me around nine tonight – I'll be all ready for you, baby. Candlelight and wine and my circular waterbed!" She gave him the sweetest smile. Then she made her way up to the front of the plane where her other admirer was breathing heavily, slipped him the key and the address and murmured, "Nine o'clock, don't be late!" I bet that first fellow felt a fool. I certainly did when I showed up at his apartment ....*

'But it's the stewardess who is our shining example. How can we fail to admire the way she disengaged herself from that unwelcome situation without actually offending anyone ....'

INTERNATIONAL COMPETITION 'Are the British sufficiently competitive? Well, the famous British reserve, that self-effacing modesty, seems to evaporate very rapidly whenever anyone suggests that another nation can boast more beautiful women.

'*A subject once discussed by an Arab, an Englishman and a Swede. The Arab said, "Arabian women are the most beautiful in the world – the sensuous walk, the demure gaze over the yashmak – why, when I leave home every day I kiss each of my wives in turn. And when I return from my day's work, only one of them is in bed waiting for me. I tell you this to show how beautifully they agree between themselves who shall enjoy my attentions." The Englishman said, "So sorry to disagree, but English women are definitely the most beautiful – the complexion of a rose, the grace, poise and style – why, when I leave home every day I give my wife a peck on the cheek. And when I return from my day's work, the house is spotless, the children are bathed and my supper is on the table. I tell you this to show you how beautifully she accomplishes her wifely duties." The Swede said, "You pardon me, but Swedish women are the most beautiful – plump, rosy-cheeked, blonde – why, when I am leaving my home every day, I am giving my wife a slap on the bottom. And when I return, the bottom is still trembling. And I tell you this not to give you the idea that Swedish women have fat bums, but to show you what a short working day we have in Sweden."*

'Patriotism takes pride in very different national assets. And companies too vary in their reasons for feeling proud ....'

NB: This is a carefully phrased and detailed story. If you decide to use it, it's necessary to study its repetitions and variations and memorise them thoroughly. With the right audience, it's a big, long laugh, the kind I put next to closing.

POSSESSIONS 'It's been said that the man who has everything is probably not married to the woman who wants everything. Such a man is widely envied today. More and more it seems that material gain is placed before spiritual. The philosophy of the Yuppie could be expressed as "I own, therefore I am."

'*I heard of one young, upwardly mobile executive in London's Dockland who was speeding in his treasured Porsche when he crashed. A constable pulled him from the blazing wreck and said, "Keep still, I'll get an ambulance." But all the Yuppie could say was, "My Porsche, my Porsche, my Porsche ....!" The policeman said, "That's the least of your worries, sunshine, you've lost your left arm." And the Yuppie said, "My Rolex, my Rolex, my Rolex ....!*'

'Worldly goods are all very well but this room is filled with an intangible though far greater wealth – good fellowship ....'

THE LEGAL MIND 'What's that cynical old definition of a lawyer? He's a man who gets two people to strip off for a fight and then runs off with their clothes. How unkind – yet it rings a bell for each of us. The legal profession could do with an improved image.

'*I'm rather fond of the classic story about the dying millionaire who called three men to his death-bed – his vicar, his doctor and his lawyer. The old man said, "They say you can't take it with you but I'm going to try. Here are three fireproof envelopes, each of them containing £50,000, one apiece. Take them and keep them until the day of my funeral – and just before they lower my coffin, throw them in with me." And so it was done on the funeral day, but on the road back in the black limousine, the vicar made a confession. He said, "I took £10,000 for the Church Restoration Fund and only threw in £40,000." The doctor said, "To be frank, I took £20,000 for new hospital equipment and only threw in £30,000." And the lawyer said, "I'm ashamed of you, gentlemen. I threw in a cheque for the full amount."'*

SELLING TOO HARD 'We have to guard against stretching the truth too far – it may snap back.

'*As in the old classic about the matchmaker who takes a young suitor to meet a prospective bride and her family. As they're leaving, the matchmaker says, "Aren't they wonderful? What an honour to become part of such a family! Cultured people, dignified, educated, full of honour and integrity – and did you see their silverware? Pure sterling!" The young man says, "Ah, but perhaps they only borrowed it to make a good impression." And the matchmaker says, "Are you crazy? Who would lend anything to those thieves?"*

'A good product doesn't sell itself, it just deserves an equally good salesman.'

RELAXATION 'Stress is not only a personal enemy, it's an enemy to good business too. A decision taken under pressure can go wrong. Let me tell you what my doctor says – it's pretty good advice when you think about it. He says the best time to relax is when you haven't got time to relax.

'*I heard of a Belfast doctor who told an overworked priest, "Go to London, put away your Roman collar, forget the church for two months and have some really relaxing fun." A week later the priest is wearing a Gaultier suit, sipping a dry Martini in the sauciest Soho Club when a cute little topless waitress says, "Hi there, Father O'Malley!" He says, "How do you know me?" She says, "I'm Sister Theresa, we go to the same doctor."*

'If the job gets one hundred per cent and there's nothing good left for you, pretty soon there's nothing good left for the job ....'

COINCIDENCE 'It's only in fiction that coincidences seem unnatural. When they occur in life, we're hardly surprised.

'*Only last week two friends of mine were walking down the street when one said, "There's my wife and my girlfriend talking to each other!" And the other one said, "Small world, isn't it?"*

'I think it's a lucky coincidence that you and I are here at the same time ....'

CURIOSITY 'In the words of Ralph Waldo Emerson, "Curiosity is lying in wait for every secret." Some mysteries are irresistible.

'*As in the classic about the honeymoon couple who bought a talking parrot in a bazaar. The damn thing kept up a running commentary on everything they were doing in bed. Finally the groom chucked a bath towel over its cage and said, "Shut up or we'll sell you to a zoo!" Next morning they were packing and couldn't get the big suitcase shut. He said, "Darling, you get on top and I'll try. No, that's not working – let me get on top and you try." She said, "That's not working either, dearest. Why don't we both get on top?" And the parrot yanked off the towel and said, "Zoo or no zoo, this I've got to see!"*

'I feel just as curious as that parrot and just as determined to know the answers that await us ....'

ANTICIPATING NEEDS 'What you need today may not be what you will need tomorrow. It's a good idea to reconsider your priorities regularly.

'*Remember the drunk weeping to his friend, "I did a terrible thing. I sold my wife to a guy for a bottle of Scotch." His friend said, "That is terrible. And now that she's gone you wish you had her back." And the drunk said, "Bloody right, I'm thirsty again."*

'He didn't anticipate requirements. I just hope that I've anticipated yours ....'

SPECIALISATION 'We should all stick to what we do best, but if what we do isn't the best, it's better not to claim credit for it.

'*There's a classic tale about three specialists – a doctor, civil engineer and a politician – all discussing the beginning of Creation. The doctor says, "It was obviously a surgical job. The Bible says Eve was made by removing a rib from Adam." The engineer says, "That came later, before that it was an engineering job. For in six days the earth was created out of chaos." "Ahah!" says the politician, "But who created the chaos?"*

'So what can we claim to have created here ....?'

ADVICE 'The best time to give advice to your children is while they're still young enough to believe you know what you're talking about. By the time they're twenty, they think you are a fool. By the time you are forty, they're surprised how much you've learned in the meantime.

'An old story but still a great one from the French film-maker Jean Renoir. He tells of the Sorbonne graduate getting some astute business advice from his old man: "My boy, guard well the fingers of your right hand." "Why, mon père?" "It's like this – the little finger extends when you drink tea – this shows class. The third finger is for the wedding ring. The middle finger is for pleasure, the index finger is for turning the pages of our financial ledgers, and the thumb is for passing judgement, up or down." The young man thought for a moment and then said, "Papa, I understand all that except the part about the middle finger being for pleasure." And the old man answered, "Think, my boy, think! How else would you punch the cash register?"

'There are a few points we can count off on *our* fingers ....'

REVENGE 'A gambling expert tells me that the longest odds in the world are those against getting even. But it's still tempting.

'Which recalls the classic instance of the two English schoolboys who were always feuding and grew up to be bitter enemies. One entered the Royal Navy and became an Admiral. The other entered the Church and in due time became a Bishop. Years later they met again on a London railway platform. The Bishop, who had grown enormously fat, walked up to the Admiral who was decked out in his full official regalia, a uniform resplendent with decorations. He said, "I say there, Stationmaster, what time does the train leave for Canterbury?" And the Admiral bowed and said, "Any minute now, madam, but in your condition you really shouldn't be travelling."

'The truth is that time spent in getting even is far better used in getting ahead ....'

FAITH 'Peter De Vries once said, "It takes a lot more faith to live this life without faith than with it." And faith, once accepted into the heart, carries the mind with it.

'Like Mrs. Murphy who said to her parish priest, "I hear you're away to Rome, Father. Would you say a prayer for me that I'll get pregnant at last and raise a wee family?" The clergyman said, "I'll do more than that, Mrs. Murphy, I'll light a candle in St. Peter's Basilica." Eight years later he returned to (name of local town) and the first soul he saw was Mrs. Murphy. She kissed his hand and said, "You're a living saint, Father. The three boys are at school, the twins are in the pram, and the two girls are playing in the yard." He said, "Glory be to God! And where's your husband?" She said, "He's gone off to Rome to blow out the candle."

'Good luck and faith may sometimes be confused but we do best when we are blessed with both ....'

CIRCUMSTANCES 'It's been said that whether circumstances make one bitter or better depends entirely on the letter "I".

'*The great American humourist Will Rogers took the better view. He was delivering one of his famous topical monologues in the great Ziegfeld Follies on an evening during World War I when a grim-looking female in the balcony screamed, "Why aren't you in the armed forces?" Rogers gazed upwards at his heckler until everyone had turned to look at her, then he drawled, "Ma'am, it's for the same reason you ain't in the Ziegfeld Follies – physical disabilities."*

'As for all of us, in sporting terms, it's "horses for courses".'

HYPOCRISY 'A hypocrite is someone who slaps you on the back in front of your face, and slaps you in the face behind your back.

'*Like the hypocritical wheeler-dealer who once told Mark Twain, "Before I kick the bucket I intend to make a pilgrimage to the Holy Land, climb to the very top of Mount Sinai and read the Ten Commandments out loud." Twain said, "I've got a better idea. Why don't you stay right here where you are and keep them?"*

'Honesty is still the best policy. Of course, there are fewer policy holders than there used to be ....'

CONCEIT 'A vain man thinks he's flattering his wife when he congratulates her on her choice of husband. Thank goodness there's always a pin for such a balloon.

'*A notoriously self-centred comedian was due to be the Guest of Honour at yet another show business dinner for one of the many charities he supports. He stood in front of the mirror in the gents' cloakroom, adjusting his black bowtie, pinching his cheeks to heighten the colour and generally checking out his appearance. Then he said to the attendant, "How many really important men do you think there are in the banqueting hall tonight?" And the attendant said, "One less than you think."*

'Looking around me, I have exactly the same feeling ....'

INTERPRETATIONS 'Whatever action we take we should always bear in mind its possible ambiguities. Can it be misunderstood? And could that misunderstanding arise from our previous behaviour?

'*About a year ago I had to complain angrily to the manageress of our local dry cleaners. I can't have left her with a very favourable impression of me. Then last week I put a red ballpoint pen in the breast pocket of my white shirt and forgot to put the cap on it. It made a ghastly scarlet stain with a dark centre all over the pocket and my wife said, "It won't wash out, I'll try the cleaners." The manageress took a long, slow look at the shirt and then looked sideways at my wife with a furtive grin and murmured, "Good shot."*

'At least let's make it clear that our aims are not criminal ....'

POSITIVE THINKING 'I've heard it said that positive something is better than negative nothing. I'm all for the power of positive thinking, but some of its optimistic language, though it trips off the tongue, can also trip you up.

'I took a computer course recently in distinguished company. Along with several leading businessmen of my age, I sat like a new boy in school and grappled with the jargon familiar to all end-users but like Martian to me. Our instructor fairly radiated positive thinking. He thought and spoke only in terms of the impossibility of failure and the certainty of success. We were given a test in data processing to complete and, as we did so, one or two of us began to discuss the problems we'd encountered. The instructor wasn't having that. He said, "Let me make one thing perfectly clear, gentlemen! In the world of computer programming there are no such things as problems – only opportunities!" There was a pause, and then a very eminent executive in the far corner said very gently, "In that case, I wonder if you'd give me some help with an insurmountable opportunity?"

'It's fine to have one eye on the objective providing you keep an objective view ....'

LATERAL THINKING 'The ability either to see a gap in the market, or to spot a dormant public demand that needs awakening, or visualise the application of a familiar tool to a new and unfamiliar task – this is the kind of thinking which breaks out of the habitual and into the unconventional. Why is it so rare? Most of us use this trick of informal figuring when we're at play – doing crosswords, playing cards, even cracking jokes. We use it whenever we solve a logical puzzle, like G-H-O-T-I spells "fish". If you don't know why G-H-O-T-I spells "fish", I'll explain in just a moment.

'This capacity for identifying unusual connections was the very test used on the final applicants for the job as head chef at the Ritz Hotel. The general manager had reduced his shortlist to three, an Englishman, a Scotsman and an Irishman. (When this joke happened the Welshman was on holiday.) He said, "Look, gentlemen, your qualifications are identical and I can't separate you, so we must use a tie-breaker. I've put three objects on this table. I want each of you to pick the odd one out and give me your reasons." And on the table were a cabbage, a potato and a knife. The English contender said, "The odd

one out is the knife because the other two are edible." The Scotsman said, "Aye, it's the knife all right but not for that reason. It's because the cabbage and the potato are vegetable and the knife is mineral." Murphy took a look and said, "It's the cabbage." "The cabbage? Why the cabbage?" "You can make chips with the other two."

'As to why G-H-O-T-I spells "fish", it's just another example of spotting the connection, this time between English spelling and pronunciation. In the word "cough" the G-H are pronounced F, "cough". In the word "women", the O is pronounced as I, "women". In the word "motion", the T-I are pronounced SH, "motion". That's an F, an I and a SH and that spells "fish". Which sends my mind leaping sideways to this thought ....'

SELFISHNESS 'The American humourist Roger Price wrote a book called *Me First*. In it he coined one of my favourite ambiguities: "When it comes to giving to others, I stop at nothing." Of course, there are certain circumstances in which total self-absorption is understandable.

'*Consider a chap called Henry whose doctor tells him he has only eight hours to live. Henry goes home in a state of shock and tells his wife, "I've only got seven hours to live." (It's taken him an hour to get home.) For the next sixty minutes, they're weeping, lamenting, then he says, "Wait a minute! I've only got six hours left – let's do something worthwhile with my last six hours." She says, "What?" He says, "Let's make love." So they go upstairs and enjoy an hour of passion. Harry's exhausted, he sleeps for an hour. They he wakes up, it's 10pm, he says, "I've got four hours left – let's make love again!" Once more sixty minutes of passion go by and once more he crashes out, shattered. He sleeps for an hour, wakes up at midnight, shakes his wife's arm and says, "I've still got a couple of hours of life left – let's make love again." And she says, "Oh come on, have some consideration! I've got to get up in the morning, you haven't."*

'In most cases, however, we best serve ourselves by putting others first, be it the family, the company or the customer ....'

ADVANCING THE CUSTOMER'S NEEDS 'In politics, the public is divided into friends and enemies. In business, they're all customers. And what a customer thinks he needs is often less than we can sell him. It's just a matter of being alert to opportunity.

'*Like the tattooist when a pretty punk rocker walked into his parlour and said, "Can you tattoo a wildcat on my knee?" And he said, "We're having a sale on giraffes this week."*

'We too should aim as high as we possibly can ....'

SPORTS CLASSICS

Every kind of sport has its comic legends and here are some stories that have proved their worth. It seems that golf attracts the greatest number of funny lines and anecdotes so 'Golfing Gags' occupies the most space. But let's kick off with:

Soccer Stories

'I was telling my son there's nothing certain in life. Then QPR lost another game. (Use the name of any well-known losing football team.) I spend a lot of my time watching that team. My doctor told me to avoid excitement. They just spent £30,000 on ground improvements – turned the seats round to face the pitch.

'We got beaten by (Luton) last Saturday. One of our players went up to the referee and said, "Can we have a new ball?" "What's wrong with the one you've got?" "Luton are playing with it."
'But we've got a winning team here today ....'

Poor old (losing FC), they're in terrible financial difficulties. They splashed out what spare money they'd got to buy the team proper club ties but I think they look pathetic. Why can't the lads have shirts and shorts like the other teams?

'They had a fire at their ground the other week. The manager panicked – he said, "It hasn't damaged the cup, has it?" They said, "No, it never even got as far as the canteen."
'But without losers, there would be no winners ....'

'The Two Ronnies had a smart little news item from Scotland: "In the Celtic versus Rangers match, fighting among the crowd was interrupted when football broke out on the pitch."

FOLLOWING A BIG MATCH 'It was sold out, of course, with the usual ticket touts trying to make a killing. I heard one punter saying, "Fifty quid for a football match? I could get a woman for that." And the tout said, "Yes, but you won't get forty-five minutes each way and a brass band in the middle."

'One of the ticket touts was Irish. You could tell because he was inside the ground. And he told me they play a lot in Ireland.

'Cork were playing Limerick and the referee came from Skibbereen. He called the two captains together before the match and said, "Look, lads, before the afternoon's over, I think it's going to get foggy, so what do you say we play the extra time first?"
'Taking a tip from that, I'll use my extra time right now ....'

'I play for our local team in (name of home town). Best result so far was losing to the senior citizens by the odd goal in thirteen. They beat us 12–nil.

'*One of our supporters is a dairy farmer who always brings along his very plain unmarried sister. I've noticed now he always likes to stand near the halfway line while she takes up her position directly behind our goal posts. Last week I asked him why his sister prefers to stand there and he said, "She b'ain't no beauty, let's be fair. And this is the only time she ever sees men running' right at 'er"*

'Like so many things, it all depends on the point of view ....'

'Mike Yarwood sympathises with Stockport. He says the team's taking art lessons so they can draw bigger crowds.

'*And they are trying to boost attendance. Before each home game they have two hundred policemen outside the ground throwing hooligans in. But I make donations to the club each season. I put one pound in an envelope and sent it off last year. I got a very nice letter back from the Chairman saying, "Thank you for the pound you sent. Which two players do you want?"*

'Why, it took nearly twice that much to lure me here tonight ....'

'My old football injury is acting up again. It happened a few years ago now. I was watching *Match of the Day* and I accidentally cut my thumb on a can of Carling's Black Label. Of course, some supporters are even more dedicated than I am.

'*One loyal (name of club) supporter went to the Club Secretary and said, "I've spent my entire life devoted to the team and I've not long to go. When that Great Referee in the Sky blows his final whistle for me, I want to be cremated. And I want my ashes scattered over the ground." The Secretary said, "Now, now, Winston, you know very well that we don't allow spectators onto the pitch. Have you thought about being mummified?" The old chap said, "What a grand idea! I'll have myself preserved and you can put me in my old seat in the stand every Saturday!" And, believe it or not, that's just what happened. He died, the taxidermist did his stuff, and there he was the following Saturday afternoon, stuffed and mummified, looking better than usual, sitting in his usual seat in the usual stand at (club) Football Ground, as usual. And the team played up to their normal standard, as usual. And he left at half-time, as usual.*

'And it's time the speaker offered his thanks, as usual ....'

KEEPING YOUR EYE ON THE BALL (AFTER A LEG-PULLING INTRODUCTION) 'I don't know. Having you warm up an audience is a little like having Yasser Arafat warm up a bagel. But in football, you learn to take a few kicks, fouls and penalties. Most importantly, as in life, you learn to take your eye off the ball. When its direction changes, you change with it. Like that classic tale I heard in Glasgow.

'This Scottish landlord is a fanatical Rangers supporter, so fanatical that he had a sign up over the bar saying "NO CELTIC FANS SERVED IN THIS PUB!" One day a bloke wearing a green and white scarf, green and white hat and green and white favour – the Celtic colours – dashes into the pub desperate for a drink. He says to the landlord, "I know you don't serve Celtic supporters but I'm dying for a pint – I'll give you a pound for one jar." He gets his pint, downs it in one and says, "Same again." The landlord says, "That'll cost ye five pounds." The bloke pays up, drinks it and asks for a third pint. "A third pint'll cost you ten pounds." When he asks for a fourth pint, it costs him fifteen pounds. He drinks it down and says, "That's better" and goes. And the landlord takes down the sign and puts up another that says: "ONLY CELTIC FANS SERVED IN THIS PUB."

'If you're not flexible to market forces, you lose profits. As in football, to win you must adapt to every changing situation ....'

Golfing Gags

'Someone defined a golf ball as a sphere made of rubber bands wound up about as tensely as the man trying to hit it. Of course, that was before they found new ways to make them. I've bought some of these 'longer distance balls'. You can't believe how much further out of bounds they'll go. To give you some idea of how they've improved my game, I've got the only caddy on the course in a snorkel and flippers.

'I'm not as bad as (name) though. He drove four successive balls into the water and then blew his top. He snatched his bag from the caddie and threw the whole lot into the pond – bag, clubs, balls and all. Then he said, "Now I'm going to jump in there and drown myself." The caddie said, "I doubt it." "What do you mean, you doubt it?" The caddy said, "You never have learned to keep your head down."

'Well, I think I can be more tactful than that ....'

'Every golfer has his excuses for playing badly, even Bob Hope. According to Radio 4's *Week Ending*, Hope blamed his disappointing stroke play in his last charity classic on a man holding the cue cards in the wrong order.

'Hope tells the story that his doctor told him he was overworked for a man in his eighties and needed a complete rest – and that included giving up golf. Hope decided to give up his doctor instead. He tried a second opinion and a third, and on the fourth try he found a doctor who told him he could play eighteen holes whenever he felt like it. Hope says he actually hugged the man and said, "Thanks, doc, just for that I'll remember you in my will." And the doctor said, "In that case, play thirty-six."

'Personally I think there's only one psychologically right time to give up golf. It's when your putt goes further than your drive. And this may be the psychologically right time to say this ....'

'Every golf ball has 332 dimples. Easy for me to remember – the way I'm playing lately that's one dimple per stroke. And when you're off form, the least thing can distract you.

'The last game I played with (name) was a bit temperamental. And as if things were tense enough, the caddie developed a deafening case of hiccups. On the sixteenth, (name) sliced his drive way out of bounds, turned to the caddie and said, "That's thanks to you and your bloody hiccups!" The caddie said, "But I didn't hiccup then, sir." (name) said, "That's just the point – I had allowed for it!"

'And now I must ask you to make allowances for me ....'

'I'm not saying (name) is a bad golfer, but he's stood in more sand than Lawrence of Arabia. When he lowers his head, he's not just putting – he's praying.

'Rather like Tony Jacklin's tale about the priest and the rabbi playing at (name of local course). The priest made a small silent prayer before each putt and he was sinking them from every corner of the green. The rabbi was rattled. Half in jest he said, "If you taught me that little prayer of yours, do you think my putts would start dropping too?" The priest said, "Frankly no." "Why not?" "Because you're a lousy putter."

'However, if you have prayers, prepare to say them now ....'

'I like to watch golfers on the links and try to figure out their relationships.

'For instance, you can always spot an employee who's playing with his boss. The employee is the player who gets a hole-in-one and says, "Oops!"

'The secret of good golf is threefold: hit the ball hard, straight, and not too often. That's fine until you find yourself playing a hole that refuses to let you do either the second or the third.

'A veteran golfer I knew at (name of local club) was constantly defeated by the 13th hole. That hole always got the better of him, always made him finish up one or two strokes over par. He told his wife, "When I die, I want to get *my own back on that 13th hole if it kills me! Promise me you'll have my ashes scattered all over that damned 13th hole."* And sure enough, when he died, after the funeral, his wife solemnly scattered his ashes all over the fairway – and the wind blew them out of bounds.'

'Sometimes you can't win – but you've got to try ....'

'Ronnie Corbett has said that his local course in Surrey is one of the toughest in England and I can't disagree. I mean, how often have you seen a sandtrap with headstones. Consequently, it attracts quite a lot of visitors who fancy a challenge.

'One out-of-town visitor finished his game and he's standing in the showers, musing on his handicap, when he hears a group of lady members outside the shower, laughing. I wish they were here tonight. Anyway, he realises that they're all getting undressed and that he's in the ladies' shower. So he covers his head with a towel, rushes out past the three women and makes his escape. The first woman said, "Who was that? It wasn't my husband." The second woman said, "No, you're right, it wasn't, and it wasn't my husband either." And the third woman said, "He isn't even a member of the club."

'It's not only a nice story, it's a relief that religion doesn't come into it. Ronnie Corbett also says nine holes are enough for him – he usually plays four and falls down five. But that's what every game is all about – the challenge ....'

'Jimmy Tarbuck says, "I used to play a lot with Ronnie Corbett but he drove me mad. Just as you're about to drive, he moves and the ball rolls off his head."

'*A caddy at Sunningdale got on Jimmy's nerves one afternoon. He said to the man, "Are you anxious to get home or what? Every time I hit the ball, you look at your watch." The caddy said, "It's not a watch, it's a compass.'*

'I get my warning signs when you look at your watches ....'

'Bruce Forsyth was in a talkative mood during a match with a tight-lipped Sean Connery. The more Bruce chattered, the quieter Sean became. Just as Sean was driving off from the 5th, Bruce launched into another topic and the ball fell short into a bunker. "Shame," said Bruce, "but there's an even worse trap than that on this course." Sean said, "I know – why don't you shut it?"

'*Sean likes the tale of Jesus and Moses coming to earth incognito to play a game at Turnberry. They're on the wrong side of the pond on a short hole and Jesus says to his caddy, "Give me a seven-iron." Moses says, "Why not? Jack Nicklaus did it" He gives it an Almighty swing, if you'll excuse the expression, and SPLOSH! The ball's in the water. He says, "Moses, do me a favour and fetch my ball." So Moses parts the waters and brings back the ball. Again Jesus lines up a shot with the seven-iron, again Moses says, "You'll never clear that pond with a seven-iron," and again Jesus says, "Why not? Jack Nicklaus did it." He swings again and SPLASH! Ball's back in the water. "Moses, fetch the ball again, please." Moses says, "No, it's your ball, you get it." So Jesus walks out onto the water. One of the caddies says, "I don't believe this game. Who does he think he is – Jesus Christ?" And Moses says, "No, Jack Nicklaus."*

'Some golfers have the perfect cure for a stiff neck: rub it with alcohol – from the inside.

'On a bitterly cold day last November four of our oldest members went out into the winds, determined not to give up their twice-weekly foursome. Off they roared from the 1st tee, repeating their pet insults, making crazy bets, stopping after each four strokes to pass round the hip flasks. By the 18th green the four of them were so sozzled their knees were bending both ways. Besides which, they were all even. The entire match depended on whether or not one of the oldest of these four alcoholic granddads could sink a fifteen-foot putt uphill. He balanced himself very gingerly and prepared to make the putt, at which point a big red fox with a bushy tail flew from behind a clump of gorse, dashed between the old fellow's legs with an earsplitting howl, leaped off into the rough and vanished. Without batting an eyelid, the old boy calmly putted his ball into the cup. The other three couldn't get over it. They congratulated him all the way back to the locker room. They said, "You're a marvel. Fancy sinking a difficult putt like that even though a damn great fox ran between your legs." And the old chap focussed his eyes and said, "Hell's teeth, you don't mean that was a real fox?"*

'Tonight, nothing's going to put me off my stroke either ....'

'That elegant funny-man Dickie Henderson said he once played eighteen holes at Palm Springs with the legendary Arnold Palmer. As the round ended, Dickie asked anxiously, "What do you think of my game?" Palmer said, "Not bad but I still prefer golf."

Dickie's favourite tale was of when he took his wife Gwyneth out for the first time. He told her to tee off and she said. "I can't – those men in front are looking at me." So Dickie yelled, "Hey, fellers! Don't look!" One of the players looked at his friend and said, "What did he say?" His friend said, "He said, 'Don't look:' and the other bloke said, "Why? What are they going to do?"'

'I once asked the late great Tommy Cooper, "What was your lowest score?" He said, "Fifty-four." "And your highest?" He said, "Two hundred and ninety-eight." I said, "What happened?" He said, "I used a ball." I said, "What's the longest ball you ever hit?" He said, "Three thousand miles. It went through the window of a plane." Despite his magical skills, Tommy confessed that he'd never attained the golfer's Holy Grail – the hole-in-one.

'Like that appalling golfer who swore, "I'd give anything for it" – and there on his shoulder appeared a tiny Devil who said, "If I grant you a hole-in-one, will you agree to give up ten years of your sex life?" This terrible golfer said, "Anything! It's my life's ambition." And with that he drove off down the fairway, his ball hit a rock, bounced off a tree, and rolled into the cup. "Let me do it again!" he yelled and the Devil said, "It'll cost you ten more years of your sex life!" "It's a deal!" – and he holed another in one at the second – and another at the third – a world record! And the Devil met him behind the clubhouse and said, "You've lost thirty years of sex, my friend, I hope it was worth it. Now for the details – what's your name?" And the golfer said, "Father O'Malley."

'I'd love to sink a ball in one but I wouldn't sacrifice this evening for it ....'

'I wasn't playing at my best the other day and the caddy I had was worse than useless. I said, "You must be the worst caddy in the world." And he said, "No, that would be too much of a coincidence." What do you tip a man like that?

'As I was leaving I said to the pro, "That caddy is a cheeky swine. You were watching my game – what do you think I should give him?" He said, "Your clubs."

'(Name) never cheats. He just makes his nines upside down. You might say he plays by numbers – he sets to, yells "Fore!", takes six and puts down five. I think fiddling his score has become too much of a habit. Last week he got a hole-in-one and put down a zero.

'And he'll make any excuse for playing off-form. I took him out to a new country club for a game the other week. I teed off, then he took a wild swing at his ball and missed by a mile. He tried again and again and each time he missed it. I was embarrassed, he wasn't. He turned to me and said, "It's a good thing I discovered this early in the game. This course is at least two inches lower than the one I usually play on."

'I have a similar problem – the IQ in this room is higher than I'm used to ....'

'I never really mean to cheat at golf. It's just that I play for my health and a low score makes me feel better. But just now and then comes that incredible stroke of luck that makes all the suffering worthwhile.

'*It would have been a real triumph except that I was playing with (name). I stepped up to the tee, drove off and got a hole-in-one. Then he stepped up to the tee and said, "Okay, now I'll take my practice swing and then we'll start the game."*

'Okay, that was my practice joke, now let's start the speech ....'

'There are two things I like to leave behind me when I walk onto the golf course – business worries and sarcasm.

'*I had an office problem on my mind last Saturday and it was ruining my form. I said to my partner, "Sorry, I'm not playing my usual game." He said, "Ah, that accounts for it – what game do you usually play?"*'

'They're saying golf is so popular it's replaced sex. Of course, it's the fellers who are over sixty who are saying it. But that's one of its joys – you can take it up at any time of life.

'*I know a workaholic, efficiency-mad businessman in (name of local town) who finally had to retire and it's driving him crazy. It's driving his wife crazy too, so to get him out of the house, she buys him a beautiful set of clubs and a membership at the local club. He presents himself to the resident pro and says, "Look, this game is a total mystery to me. What do I have to do?" The pro says, "See that flag down there on the green? You hit the ball towards that flag." The man picks out a club at random, swipes at the ball and by some miracle of chance it goes straight down the middle and rolls across the green till it stops two inches from the hole. The pro can't believe his eyes. The man says, "What next?" The pro gulps and says, "You're supposed to hit the ball into the cup." And the businessman says, "Now he tells me!"*

'Well, I think we're unexpectedly lucky too ....'

'Mad about golf? If they were going to hang him, he'd ask the executioner to let him take a couple of practice swings.

'*Once in Scotland I played with the most fanatical golfer I've ever met. We were just teeing off on the 15th where the green lies next to the main road. He was in the middle of his backswing when a row of funeral cars came past. He stopped, took off his cap, held it over his heart and bowed his head. I was impressed. I said, "You're a man who shows real respect for the deceased." He said, "It's only fair. She was a good wife to me for 37 years."*

'That's one kind of dedication. I'd like to make another ....'

'In school we have the rule of three, in courtship the rule of two, in marriage the rule of one ... and in golf, quite a number of unwritten rules. But everyone plays by them.

'*I was in the locker room at (local) Golf Club when the old attendant there answered the phone. He heard a female voice say, "Is my husband there?" He said, "No, lady, 'e's not 'ere." She yelled, "How can you can he's not there when I haven't even told you my name?" And he said, "Don't make no difference, lady. There ain't never nobody's 'usband 'ere!"*

'It's a poor rule that won't work both ways. And an even poorer one that won't work our way ....'

Horse Racing

'In horse racing there's nothing as uncertain as a sure thing. And if you think there is, chances are you'll wind up getting nothing for something. Funny thing is though, every horse trainer and every bookie has a story about racing coincidences.

'*I was at Kempton Park for the Jubilee Handicap, having a quiet pint in the Old Swan, when I noticed three racehorses sitting in a corner of the snug, drinking shandy and reminiscing. The first one said, "I was in the 5.15 at Warwick last month, lying fifth and not bothered, when a dog barked somewhere and startled me so much I put on a spurt and won by a length." The second horse said, "What a coincidence! I was taking it easy in the 2 o'clock at Haydock Park when the same thing happened. A dog barked, gave me a start and I shot ahead to win by a head." The third horse said, "I can't get over this! Didn't exactly the same thing happen to me in the 4.30 at Doncaster? I was noodling along in the rear – woof woof! I jumped so much I led the field and came in at eight to one." Listening to all this was a greyhound, sipping a port and lemon. It sauntered over to the three horses and said, "You're not going to believe this, but only last night I was running at Brighton, the back marker, when suddenly I heard a horse whinny! It gave me such a shock I leapt into the lead!" And the first racehorse turned to the others and said, "Isn't that incredible? A talking dog!"*

'I'm sorry, I'm afraid I've been lying to you. This actually happened at Newmarket in the Red Lion ....'

Boxing

'The chains of habit are too weak to be felt until they become too strong to be broken.

'*Like the old insomniac boxer who was allergic to sleeping pills. The doctor said, "The old remedies are best. Just relax and start counting to a thousand." The old boxer was back a week later. He said, "It's no use, doctor, I keep jumping up at the count of nine."*

'First we make our habits – and then our habits make us ....'

Short thoughts

If brevity is the soul of wit, these lines should provide every speaker with soul-food. None of them is offered as a knee-slapping bellylaugh. Their merit lies in their encapsulation of a truth, a smart observation or a humorous example and they are intended to promote smiles and nods rather than helpless mirth. Mind you, the occasional jokey joke sneaks in. I've used them to open a subject or wrap one up, and you'll find other applications, I'm sure. A Sales Director told me, 'I need short and intelligent lines to sprinkle over my speech like sultanas in a cake.' If you're reading this, Dickie – happy sprinkling!

Advertising

Some of it doesn't make sense, like a falsie manufacturer advertising 'Beware of Imitations'.

I keep seeing ads for mouthwashes that guarantee to kill all germs. Who wants a mouthful of dead germs?

I have a friend in Public Relations whose honeymoon was a disaster. He just sat on the edge of the bed and told her how wonderful it was going to be.

Advice

I can offer lots of advice, good advice. Advice that's been passed down from generation to generation and never been used.

Don't try to keep up with the Joneses. Drag them down to your level, it's cheaper.

If you have a jar with a lid that's stuck, do you know the easiest way to get it open? Put it on the table and tell the kids to leave it alone.

If you can't give up sex, get married and taper off.

Age

It's so unfair. You no sooner get used to being middle-aged and you're old.

You know you're getting older when you decide to procrastinate but never seem to get around to it.

I tried life in the fast lane recently. Got a summons for obstructing traffic.

Denis Norden said it: 'You know you're getting older when a four-letter word for something pleasurable two people can do in bed is R-E-A-D.'

Argument

There's one sure way to stop a red-hot argument. Drop one cold fact on it.

My wife and I have resolved not to go to bed angry. As of now we've been awake three weeks.

Some say avoid arguments if possible. I say avoid them if impossible.

There are two sides to every argument until you take one.

Art

I told (name) I didn't understand modern art and he said it's easy. If it hangs on a wall, it's a painting and if you can walk round it, it's a sculpture.

I heard one woman in the gallery say, 'That's a beautiful painting,' and the woman next to her turned and said, 'Oh, are you a relative too?'

An artist is known by the critics he praises.

Our local pub's full of artists but none of them can paint.

Average

I'd consider myself an average man if it weren't for the fact that I consider myself an average man.

On average at age eight-five there are sixty per cent more women than men. But at that age, who cares?

Babies

There was a record number of births in (name of local town) this year apparently due to the Irish Sweep ... but now he's moved back to Londonderry.

A baby's like a new car. It has two-lung power, free squealing, screamlined body, changeable seat covers and an easily flooded carburettor.

She's not a great thinker. She keeps having a baby every year because she doesn't want the youngest one to get spoiled.

Training babies is mostly a matter of pot luck.

Bachelors

I said, 'Dad, should I marry a girl who can take a joke?' He said, 'Son, that's the only kind you'll get.'

He's been single for years. Can't find someone who loves him as much as he does.

He's a very lonely bachelor. Goes to women's prisons and volunteers for conjugal visits.

She reckons no man is good enough for her. She may be right. And she may be left.

Beds

Nothing makes a lumpy mattress more comfortable than the ringing of an alarm clock.

Politics doesn't make strange bedfellows, marriage does.

The best time to put your children to bed is when you can.

My wife used to walk in her sleep, then we got a waterbed. Now she swims in her sleep.

Books

I know a publisher who begged (name of Hollywood beauty) to write her memoirs. She said, 'Submit an outline and a couple of chapters and I'll think about it.'

Never judge a book by its movie.

He said, 'This encyclopaedia will do half your work for you.' I said, 'Wonderful, I'll take two.'

I was swindled last week – I bought a book called *How To Make It Big*. It was all about money.

Budget

These days the government spends as much accidentally as it did on purpose years ago.

We posted the boss a 20-page report fastened with a paperclip. He sent back a memo: 'We don't pay to send ironmongery by airmail.'

The good news is that the Budget is doing a lot for small businesses. Bad news: these small businesses used to be big businesses.

Today people are finding out that one can live as cheaply as two.

Business

Overheard at a shareholders' meeting: 'Let's go. Whenever they fill in their speeches with little jokes, there isn't going to be a dividend.'

He told me his company's products go all round the globe. I've just found out he makes lampshades.

The company is like one big happy family. The boss hires all his relatives.

The boss told me, 'This is just a suggestion. You don't have to follow it unless you want to keep your job.'

It's an old firm. No Xerox, just a monk with a quill.

Cars

What I want is a new car with a warranty that lasts as long as the payments.
You can always tell an Italian car. They pinch your bottom.
It cost me £60 to have my car overhauled. I was speeding on the M1 when the police car overhauled it.
An old battered car travels the streets of Liverpool carrying a sign that says, 'Attention – winner in Twelve Crashes'.
The conversation turned to : 'What's the most frightening sound you can think of? One said, 'A groan in the dark when you think you're alone.' Another said, 'The slither of a black mamba in the grass.' Finally the oldest of us growled, 'I know a sound worse than all of yours put together. A long, low whistle coming from a mechanic underneath your car.'

Charm

Charm is the ability to make somebody think both of you are pretty wonderful.
Charm is what everybody notices if you've got it and nobody notices if you haven't.

Children

Kids are a comfort in your old age – and they help you reach it faster as well.
It seems a shame that most parents weren't given their neighbours' children, because those are the only ones they know how to raise.
Children – they never put off till tomorrow what will keep them from going to bed tonight.
They should make great waiters when they grow up, they never come when you call them.
If you really want your kids to do what you say ... say nothing.

Christmas

When the main difference between a man and a boy is the price of his toys.
It's that time when even the strongest of men get emotional over family ties – especially if they have to wear them.
When the Bishop of Chester said there should be a religious message on Christmas stamps, *Punch* suggested 'Lord deliver us'.
I feel strange using my credit card at Christmas – buying this year's gifts with next year's money.

Countryside

Consider the pitiful case of the chap who wants to live in the country. He's moved out three times and each time the town has overtaken him.

A city lad had spent his first night on the farm. The morning's activity woke him at four o'clock and he sat at breakfast half asleep and said, 'It doesn't take long to stay here all night, does it?'

My four-year-old son coaxed Grandpa into letting him ride on the tractor during the ploughing. Later Grandma asked, 'What were you doing in the field?' and he said. 'I don't know whether we're taking the earth out or putting it back – but we're making it wider.'

Criticism

If you want to avoid criticism, SAY NOTHING, DO NOTHING and BE NOTHING.

Never mind criticism. Most knocking is done by those who don't know how to ring the bell!

Cynicism

Instead of cursing the darkness, I lit one small candle and my fire insurance went up forty per cent.

My grandfather used to say, 'If you keep your head above the surface, you can see the stars!' Mind you, he wasn't a philosopher ... he was a sewage worker.

There's only one sure way of reducing violence. Kill everybody.

There's only one way to grow old gracefully. You've got to die young.

Dance

I never dance on any empty stomach unless it's someone I don't like.

She came to the fancy dress ball completely nude except for a cross marked on each bosom. Said she was a chest of draws.

The difference between a cha-cha and pea-green paint is that anyone can learn to cha-cha.

We did the Politician's Polka – that's one step forward, two steps back, then you sidestep the issue, open your mouth and put your foot in it.

Death

We all have to go sometime. I usually go during the commercials.

Woody Allen said it: 'I don't want to achieve immortality through my work. I want to achieve it through not dying!'

Debt

If you want to lose your shirt, keep putting too much on the cuff.

The thing that leads most people into debt, is trying to keep up with the people already there.

Definitions

Genius is a promontory jutting out into the future.

Contentment is the smother of invention.

A Yawn is nature's way of letting a husband open his mouth.

Conscience is that small inner voice that warns you when somebody's watching.

Business is what, when you don't have any, you go out of.

Falsies: the bust that money can buy.

Incest: rolling your own.

Taxi Meter: device for showing you how fast you aren't getting there.

His: pronoun which means hers.

Ramparts: these are only of interest to a sheep.

Reunion: a lot of people getting together to see who's falling apart.

Optimist: a father who lets his teenage son borrow the car. Pessimist: one who won't. Pedestrian: one who did.

Diets

I'd have no objection to people who eat like sparrows if they'd only stop that everlasting chirping about it.

I'm on a food-free diet.

She's on a sea-food diet. Only has to see food and she eats it.

There's a new Chinese diet. Order all the food you want but use only one chopstick.

If you're thin, don't eat fast. And if you're fat, don't eat ... fast!

Dirty

When a BR inspector made his annual visit to our local station, he was horrified by the dirt. He shouted, 'Look at that ticket counter! The dust's so thick I could write my name in it.' And our stationmaster said, 'So you could, but don't forget, you're an educated man.'

What a housekeeper! All her broom handles have moss growing on the North side.

Ronnie Corbett says his wife's not very houseproud: 'We're probably the only family in our neighbourhood with their Christmas decorations up all year round.'

Disagreement

These days the only people who listen to both sides of an argument are the neighbours.

If you really want the last word in an argument, try saying, 'I expect you're right.'

Divorce

My wife would divorce me tomorrow if she could find a way to do it without making me happy.

My first wife was a clever housekeeper. When we divorced, she kept the house.

Divorce is too expensive. What I need is a wife transplant.

Dogs

'No wonder the collie is half asleep,
He earns his lolli by counting sheep.'

I've got a dog that barks all night for no reason. I'm thinking of buying him a burglar.

She said, 'Rex is just like one of the family.' And without thinking I said, 'Really? Which one?'

Our dog has an ingrown tail. The only way I can find out if he's happy is to have him X-rayed.

Driving

The best safety device in a car is a rear-view mirror with a police car in it.

Drive carefully. The other bloke's car may not be paid for either.

They say if you drink, don't drive … I don't even putt.

Be very careful parking. Accidents cause people.

My wife's driving is improving. Now she runs into cheaper cars.

Drunk

One of our town characters was dragged into (name of local town) Police Station, shouting, 'What's the charge?' The sergeant said, 'You were brought in for drinking.' And the chap said, 'Oh, that's different – when do we start?'

I never knew my father drank till one night he came home sober.

They called my uncle 'the town drunk' – which isn't so bad until you realise the town was Glasgow.

I get dizzy after one drink. Usually the fifteenth.

He's a good health fanatic. Twenty times a day he says, 'Good health!'

Why worry about tomorrow when today is so far off?

There's more to life than meets the mind.

Reality is just a figment of your imagination.

Easter

When I asked my 12-year-old son what he was going to give up for Lent, he said without hesitation, 'My New Year's resolutions.'

Ted Rogers says spring is the time for all you younger chaps to get at it and court – but don't get caught at it.

I spotted my first robin, and vice versa.

Economy

Funny word, 'economy'. It means the large size in coffee and the small size in cards.

Economy, The

I'm beginning to suspect God created the world as a tax loss.

Times are so hard that people who don't intend to pay aren't buying.

I phoned my stockbroker and Dial-a-Prayer answered.

The Chancellor knows it's serious. Sometimes he lies awake at work, worrying about it.

The Strong take it from the Weak and the Brainy take it from the Strong and the Government takes it from all of us.

Exaggeration

An exaggeration is only a truth that lost its temper.

Experience

For every man who speaks from experience there's a wife who isn't listening.

Faith

One person with a belief is equal to a force of ninety-nine who only have interests.

You can't do much with faith – and you can't do much without it.

Remember, nothing is impossible as long as you don't have to do it yourself.

Nothing's impossible, although I've never seen a worm that could fall over.

Fame

One thing's sure about stardom. It doesn't come in a twinkle.

Fame is when a madman thinks he's you.

Footprints in the sands of time aren't made by sitting down.

Fashions

Overheard in a dress shop: 'My measurements are small, medium, and large – in that order.'

Most husbands want their wives to wear their dresses longer – about two years longer.

I have firm ideas about my wife's clothes ... I hate to see her in anything over twenty quid.

Fashion news – no change in men's pockets this year.

Slits in women's skirts come in three different lengths – high, higher, and 'Not guilty, your honour.'

Friendship

Identify your friends by their enemies.

Gardening

Old gardeners never die – they just spade away.

Anyone who uses a motor mower before noon on Saturday should have to shave with it.

Remember – the family that rakes together, aches together.

I haven't got green fingers. We've got a rock garden and last week three of them died.

Gifts

Ever since Eve gave Adam the apple there's been a misunderstanding between the sexes about gifts.

There are two kinds of people, the givers and the takers. The takers eat well. The givers sleep well.

Girls, Beautiful

I wouldn't trust her very far ... and she wouldn't trust me very near.

She's the kind of girl you could take home to Mother ... provided, of course, you can trust your father.

Men *do* make passes at girls who wear glasses – it all depends on their frames.

A lovely woman in a low-cut gown passed us and I said, 'Now don't start entertaining evil thoughts.' And (name) said, 'I'm not, they're entertaining me.'

Girls, In General

Why do girls who wear wigs, false eyelashes, and falsies always complain there are no real men any more?

The first thing I notice about an attractive woman is whether my wife is around.

Many a girl who says no expects to be held for further questioning.

She's a very quiet girl and she likes quiet things ... like the folding of money.

She said. 'I adore men who make things. How much do you make?'

Gossip

The woman who doesn't gossip has no friends to speak of.
Some people never get interested in anything until it's none of their business.
I hate to spread gossip, but what else can you do with it?
She can talk for two hours on what not to do if whatever might be doesn't happen.

Gratitude

Don't bite the hand that feeds you. There's more meat further up.
If your wife doesn't treat you as she should, be thankful.

Happiness

When you make two people happy, one of them is apt to be you.
You always know which people have found life a bed of roses; you hear them complaining about the thorns.
Robert Frost said happiness makes up in height what it lacks in length.
Happiness is a halfway station between too much and too little.

Health

Nobody is sicker than the man who is sick on his day off.
My doctor told me, 'No more wine and women but sing all the songs you want.'
You can tell how healthy a man is by what he takes two at a time – pills or stairs.
The picture of health requires a happy frame of mind.

Health Food

Glamour is an inside job.
Ah, there's nothing like wholesome cooking, and that's what my wife serves up – nothing like wholesome cooking.
Health foods are nothing new. When we were kids my mother served us health food ... if you knew what was good for your health, you ate the food.

Hippies

The hippie is going the way of the American buffalo, to which he bears a strong resemblance.

History

If it's true that history repeats itself, where are those 1950 prices?
Nothing makes you feel your age more than discovering your children's history lessons are what you studied as current events.

Voltaire said it – history is nothing but a pack of tricks we play upon the dead. And George Bernard Shaw said, 'We learn from history that we learn nothing from history.'

Horse-racing

You can still make a lot of money at the races, if you happen to be a horse.

You don't see me at the races throwing my money about. I've got a Government to support.

A horse is something that can run like hell until you bet twenty quid he can.

The horse I bet on came eighth but I was proud of him; it took seven other horses to beat him.

I bet on a horse that got a ticket for parking.

House and Home

Groucho Marx said, 'Home is where you hang your head.'

Ted Ray said home is the one place where whatever itches, you can scratch it.

There's no place like home, especially when you're looking for trouble.

Home: that's where he runs the show but she writes the script.

I've sold my house. The Council will go mad.

My neighbour has no civic pride. I swear his front lawn would never get cut if it weren't for my sheep.

Hunting

The judge said, 'Why did you shoot at your hunting companion, Herr Merkel?' 'I mistook him for a deer.' When did you note your error?' 'When the deer shot back.'

Paddy and Mick went hunting, saw a sign by the road: 'BEAR LEFT', so they went home.

My uncle once followed some tracks into a cave and shot a train.

If your gun is loaded, you mustn't be.

My friend said, 'I left it to you to bring all the provisions, and you bring a loaf of bread and seven bottles of booze. Now what the hell are we going to do with all that bread?

Hurry

There are two things a man likes a woman to do in a hurry – dress and undress.

The man who hasn't time to waste on a red light always finds time to attend the funeral.

It's amazing how, when I haven't enough time to do a job properly, I always have enough time to do it over again.

Husbands

If there's one thing that makes a husband angrier than his wife refusing to tell him where the money went, it's her telling him.

Ladies, why is it the same husband who forgets your birthday never forgets your age?

He always knows the short cut that takes two hours longer.

But he doesn't trust his wife's driving until the kids have to be taken somewhere.

Husbands, let your wife know that you think about her occasionally ... grind your teeth.

I'm what's known as a suburban husband. That's an oddjob man with occasional sex privileges.

Inspiration

Edward B. Newill, Vice President of General Motors, said this: 'Let us recognise a basic truth. Success in life is not a destination. It is a journey. Fortunately, this means that no-one is obliged to work towards a single distant goal and be judged successful only if he attains that one objective. As with a traveller, the end of the journey is usually beyond the range of vision, but there is much of interest and beauty along the way to reward each day's steps. The happiest journey is not made with downcast eyes which see only tired, dusty feet. It is made with uplifted sight to appreciate its significance and to picture what may lie beyond. The stars were made for those who look up and whose imagination knows no limitations.'

When I'm feeling sorry for myself I simply go for a walk. And I keep right on walking and walking, looking around me as I go – at the front doors that hide other people's fears and joys, at the marvels of nature, at the courage and invention behind every church and factory, at the sheer size and complexity of the small part of the world my legs can cover – and if that doesn't make my worries seem insignificant by comparison, I get rat-arsed!"

Insurance

My insurance man's asking far too much for the premium; last week he asked for it four times.

According to actuarial tables, people who live the longest are rich relatives.

An insurance agent is the only man who likes to see a girl fully covered.

Unbelievable, but I heard of a burglar who broke into Allied Dunbar and escaped without buying a policy.

Japan

Where else can a girl win a Beauty Contest and measure 18–12–18?

Ken Dodd says everything in Japan is miniaturised – and the women are none too pleased about it.

A full evening with a Japanese hostess comes to only £50; batteries are extra.

Jealousy

It's the blister of the heel of love.

Remember the man who didn't make love to his wife for ten years and then shot the man who did.

And the man on the flying trapeze who caught his wife in the act.

My first wife ran away with my best friend, whoever the hell he is.

Jealousy is a wife saying, 'This seat belt's been tightened, who is she?'

Jewish

International authors were asked to write about elephants. The Englishman wrote, 'The Elephant and How to Hunt It'. The Italian wrote, 'The Elephant and How to Cook It'. The Frenchman wrote, 'The Elephant and Sex'. The German wrote 14 volumes called 'The Elephant – An Introduction.' And the Israeli distributed 500,000 leaflets headed 'The Elephant and the Jewish Problem.'

My friend is half Jewish and half Gypsy ... what he can't buy wholesale, he steals.

Mrs. Cohen calls on a private detective: 'I want you should follow my husband's mistress. I want to know in detail what she sees in him.'

Kindness

The kindness planned for tomorrow doesn't count today.

Well, like they say, we're all in this world to help others. What I want to know is – what the hell are the others here for?

Kissing

Stealing a kiss sometimes leads to marriage, a perfect example of crime and punishment.

A kiss: something that brings two people so close together that they can't see what's wrong with each other.

Knowledge

There's nothing as stupid as an educated man if you get him off the subject he was educated in.

Lateness

Rushing into the lift, I bumped into my boss. He said, 'Late again!' and I heard myself saying, 'Yes, me too.'

A teenage temp arrived late in my office and she said, 'I'm sorry but a young man followed me from the bus stop.' I said, 'And that took you all this time?' And she said, 'Well, he walked so slowly.'

When I put my key in the front door I wonder what I'm letting myself in for.

Listen, if your wife no longer cares how late you come home, it's later than you think.

Law

My lawyer was attending a funeral. I arrived and took a seat beside him: 'How far has the service gone?' He nodded toward the clergyman in the pulpit and whispered back, 'He just opened the defence.'

I sent my Counsel a message from the court, 'Justice has prevailed.' He wired back, 'Appeal at once.'

If you must take the law into your own hands, strangle a solicitor.

The prisoner said, 'As God is my judge, I am innocent.' The judge: 'He's not, I am, and you're not.'

It's easy to tell right from wrong. Wrong is more fun.

You've heard of Murphy's Law, and Parkinson's Law, but have you ever heard of Cole's Law? No? It's just shredded cabbage and salad cream.

Lazy

You can take the day off but you can't put it back.

In the space marked 'Position Desired', one job applicant wrote, 'Sitting'.

(Name) will never be replaced by a computer. Where can you find a computer that does nothing?

He was off work again with his leg ... the second leg of the Darts Match.

Laziness travels so slowly, poverty soon overtakes it.

Lies

The man who has never lied to the woman he loves probably has trouble communicating with members of the opposite sex.

Life

Life is like a shower. One wrong turn and you're in hot water.

Henry de Montherlant said. 'The laws of life are founded on necessity, its charms on the non-essentials.'

Life is like a taxi. The meter keeps running whether you're going anywhere or not.

If I had my life to live over again, I wouldn't have the strength.

Ah, the simple pleasures. They do your back no good but I like'em.

A magazine once ran a competition for a statement of a philosophy of life that could be put on a postcard. The winner: 'Love, trust, dare – and keep on doing it.'

Life is like a cultivated mushroom. As soon as you put your head above the ground, someone heaps another load of fertiliser on it.

Losing your temper

Keep raising the roof and people will think there's something wrong in your attic.

Henry Link wrote, 'Becoming thoroughly angry with people is often a stage in getting to know them. If we successfully pass this point and reach the stage of hilarious laughter, we have gone far in cementing friendship.'

Love

Always remember the heart is only a muscle – so when you're in love, you're not really in love – you're muscle-bound.

Disraeli said it: 'The magic of first love is our ignorance that it can ever end.'

Love is blind. That's why you see so many spectacles in the park.

Love is the delusion that one man differs from another. (For men: 'that one woman' ....)

Take love out of sex and all you're left with is X-Certificate aerobics.

Luck

The luckiest man I know: his grandfather died, left him a fortune, he went to bury him and struck oil.

'I'm grateful for my bad luck. Without it, I could never explain my mistakes.

Sometimes a man doesn't know how lucky he is. I don't have that problem because my wife keeps telling me all day long.

Mankind

If you thought you were the only human being left on earth, how would you be sure? Do you know how? Get out a pack of cards and start playing a game of patience. If there's anyone else alive they'll be tapping you on the shoulder in a couple of minutes and saying, 'That five goes on that six.'

Man is put here to help man. Only a few months ago a friend of mine was having money trouble so, of course, I helped him out. He wept, he said, 'I'll never forget you' – and he didn't. He's in trouble again and he just called me.

Marriage

It's an investment that pays dividends if you pay interest.

Or it's just another union that defies management.

A successful marriage involves falling in love many times – always with the same person.

A cynical friend of mine says, 'Marrying a woman for her beauty is like buying a house for its paint.'

A marriage counsellor I know ushers couples in with the words, 'Think of my office as a demilitarised zone.'

Marriage is a sort of graduation ceremony in which a man loses his Bachelor's Degree without acquiring a Master's.

If you've got half a mind to get married, that's all it takes.

When a husband's words are sharp, it may be from trying to get them in edgeways.

Medicine

Medical science has developed so amazingly in recent years that it's now almost impossible for a doctor to find anything about a patient that's all right.

We're born with medical assistance and most of us die the same way.

Every hospital has two kinds of patients ... those who are ill and those who complain about the food.

John Junkin saw a hospital notice: 'Ring Bell Once If You Need Anything, Twice If It's Urgent, Three Times If It's Too Late.'

Mediocrity

Only the mediocre are always at their best.

Meditation

My father taught me to meditate. He said, 'Sit down and shut up!'

Sitting thinking the other night ... it was late, TV was over, my wife had gone to bed and I was just sitting there finishing my nightcap ... sewing the tassel on actually ....

At least when you're not doing anything and you're *not* watching TV, you know you're not doing anything.

Memory

There is a difference between not thinking of someone and forgetting him.

I went to see a doctor about my failing memory. He made me pay in advance.

Women love nostalgia. My wife loves to delve into the past and say things like, 'Where the hell were you last night?'

Middle Age

Middle age is when you get enough exercise just avoiding people who think you should have more.

You know you're middle-aged when the only thing you feel like exercising is caution.

When, instead of going on forty, you're going on Valium.

When you avoid going into antique shops in case someone makes an offer for you.

I admit it, I'm pushing fifty; got tired of pulling forty.

Modesty

It's easy to be humble when you're a success. The trick is to be arrogant when you're a flop.

Remember, a man is never so tall as when he stoops to shake hands with a chihuahua.

Money

Money in the bank is like toothpaste – easy to get it out, very hard to put it back.

The last time my wife borrowed money from me she said, 'I'll pay you back on Friday when I get your pay packet.'

It's sad to see people squandering money and know you can't help them.

There are so many things more important than money ... the trouble is, they all cost money.

Always borrow from a pessimist ... he never expects to get it back.

Money is a constant worry. But our Government is working night and day to relieve us of this worry.

Narrow-minded

A puritan is somebody who never got over the embarrassing fact that he was born in bed with a woman.

She's so narrow-minded her ears touch.

He won't sleep with his wife because she's a married woman.

She won't let the dentist in her mouth until the third appointment.

Nature

Nature usually evens things up. A grasshopper is lazier than a bee but has better manners.

Pascal said it: 'Nature is an infinite sphere whose centre is everywhere and whose circumference is nowhere.'

My brother says he's completely happy with the earth as his pillow and the sky as his blanket. He hasn't found peace of mind, he's lost his flat.

A hen is only an egg's way of making another egg.

Navy

My job aboard ship was to polish the brass. I had the shiniest captain in the fleet.

I remember when all the nice girls loved a sailor ... now it's all the nice boys.

They found the *Titanic*. Now there's an Irish salvage crew out there searching for the iceberg.

She thinks a naval destroyer is a hula hoop with a nail in it.

Newspapers

Classified ad: 'Local firm seeking attractive girl or woman with shorthand, typing and fling.'

From an ad for a sale of postage stamps in Cardiff: 'The British Empire will be disposed of in the morning, Southern Ireland remaining until after lunch.'

The Sun is called yellow journalism, especially if you put it under your puppy.

New Year

My New Year's Eve couldn't have been duller if I were Adam.

New Year's Eve advice: Remember, if you drink, don't drive. And if you drive, don't park too close to the kerb. I might be lying there.

I went to a Gay Nineties Party. All the men were gay and all the women were ninety.

Last New Year's Day, I felt as if I'd been using a trampoline in a ship's cabin.

Me and the Old Year usually pass out at the same time.

Office, The

I've never forgotten seeing three labels in a Government office: 'URGENT', 'FRANTIC' and 'PASSING INTO LEGEND'.

The Managing Director and I never disagree. He simply goes his way and I go his.

Originality

To be exactly the opposite is also a form of imitation.

Originality is rare. Most of us know a good thing as soon as the other fellow sees it.

My secretary has unique ideas but they're entirely confined to spelling.

Don't expect anything original from an echo.

Pain

I like Zsa Zsa Gabor's remark: 'I went to this gigantic party, darling, but it was so dull, I was the only one there I'd ever heard of.'

Why is it that the ones who want to leave early and the ones who want to stay late are always married to each other?

I don't go to parties much. Only when I'm invited.

Perspective

Everything's relative. There's this man, 98 years old, and he broke a mirror. Now he's overjoyed that he's going to have seven years' bad luck.

It's all in how you look at it. Dawn can be the beginning of a new day or the end of a big night!

Philosophy

My granddad left me with a great piece of philosophy. You can have money, lose money, you'll get new money. You can have love, lose love, you'll get new love. But if you lose your sense of humour, then you lose everything. In that respect, I can assure you that this audience has nothing to worry about.

I think I exist; therefore I exist, I *think*.

Today is the first day of the rest of your life ... unless you're using a Hebrew calendar ... then today is Sunday and tomorrow's Saturday.

It matters not if you let money slip through your fingers. Or even if you let love slip through your fingers, But if you let your fingers slip through your fingers, you're really in trouble.

Politics

MPs should always remember that they have to live with their consciences longer than they do with their constituents.

Politics makes estranged bedfellows.

It's been said that politics is the conduct of public affairs for private advantage. So don't avoid politics because it's full of hypocrites. There's always room for one more.

Truce is stranger than friction.

Pollution

You know you've got a pollution problem when you take a bath and the water leaves a ring round *you*.

There's only one sure way to get rid of toxic waste ... disguise it as a radio-cassette player and leave it in an unlocked car in Liverpool.

Positive Thinking

In the words of Ken Dodd: 'Think positive, men! Say, "I can and I will! I can and I will! – and she'll say, "You will if I let you! You will if I let you!"'

Cheer up! We may be worse off than we were yesterday, but we're better off than we'll be tomorrow.

Poverty

They say it's better to be poor and happy than rich and miserable. But couldn't something be worked out? Such as being moderately rich and just moody?

I was once so poor I used to buy a pint of milk for breakfast and a loaf of bread for lunch, and eat them for supper.

I wasn't born in a log cabin but my family moved into one as soon as they could afford it.

Being poor has its advantages. Your car keys, for instance, are never in your other trousers.

Prayers

Don't pray for lighter burdens, pray for stronger backs.

Sudden prayers make God jump.

Lord, grant the world patience. And I want mine now.

Prices

If you think the cost of living is high, try dying and see what it costs you.

Always be wary of the salesman who says you can't take it with you – because he's planning to take yours with him.

There's a bright side to inflation. I'm paying more in tax today than I ever dreamed of earning when I was young.

They say inflation's been beaten but I've never known a time when cheap was so expensive.

Proverbs

When in doubt, worry.

Do unto others as you would have them do unto you ... unless you're a masochist.

Ken Dodd said it: 'The best things in life are free – as the Scotsman said when he stood over a baker's grating.'

Love your enemies. It'll confuse the hell out of 'em.

Cast your bread upon the waters – but make sure the tide's coming in.

Make little things count. Teach arithmetic to dwarfs.

Punctuality

The trouble with being punctual is that no-one else is there to appreciate it.
The trouble with being punctual is that people think you have nothing better to do.
Punctuality is the art of guessing how late the other fellow's going to be.
Time is money. My, how time flies!

Questions

Why do missing teeth look so appealing in children and so unpleasant in us?
There are two sides to every question – so why is there only one answer?
Why is there such a difference between an event we can never forget and an event we will always remember?
Ever notice how with some people, the more questions they ask, the fewer answers they remember?
Since time began, men have been asking that age-old question. And wives have been replying, 'Not tonight, dear, I've got a headache.'

Radio

Radio is a kind of television perfected to the point that only sound need be transmitted.
Radio One doesn't exactly cater to the sophisticated. There's a new programme called *Whistle Something Simple* for people who can't remember the words.
Speaking on radio for money is like joining a monastery to meet girls.

Rich

The futility of riches is stated very plainly in two places, the Bible and the income tax form.
A wealthy oil sheikh wrote his first letter to St. Nicholas: 'Dear Santa, If there's anything you want for Christmas, just ask.'
There are two ways to get rich quick – marry money or divorce it.
He's so rich he has a parrot that says, 'Polly wants a croissant.' His answering machine has an answering machine. He hires Vidal Sassoon to cut his grass. Every morning he gets up and jogs for half a mile – from his bedroom to the kitchen.

Salesmanship

The customer greeted the salesman, 'This telemessage came for you.' The salesman read it and groaned, 'Oh no! My wife has presented me with twins.' And the customer said, 'Good, now you know how it feels to receive more goods than you order.'
Is he good? He could sell Father's Day cards in a home for unwed mothers.

School

My daughter's away at school for the first time. She wrote to her mother, 'Please send me some stamps, they're so expensive here.'

What a great education system we have today. Those who can, do. Those who can't, teach. And those who can't teach, teach.

Teachers today have their hands full. They have to hold chalk, a cane, a ruler, books, a loaded revolver ....

Know why they call it corporal punishment? Because across your backside, you get two stripes.

Sex

Diamonds are a girl's best friend and a dog is a man's best friend. Now you know which sex has more sense.

Rhinoceros horn is supposed to be an aphrodisiac so I tried some. All I get is this occasional urge to charge at Land Rovers.

Remember, sex is not the answer. Sex is the question. *Yes* is the answer.

A woman shows her age first thing in the morning ... a man last thing at night.

To go together is blessed. To come together is divine.

Woman lies to man. Man lies to woman. But the best part is when they lie together.

A great philosopher once said that men and women should put their differences behind them. Sounds either physically impossible or bloody agony.

Shopping

There are eight reasons why a woman buys something. Because – her husband says she can't have it, it will make her look young, it will make her look thin, her friends couldn't afford it, nobody has one, everybody has one, it's on special offer – and the eighth and most important reason of all – *because*.

My mother likes to shop in those large shopping malls. I've only just found out why. When she gets tired she can soak her feet in the fountain.

I became separated from my wife in (local department store) so I went up to an attractive salesgirl and said, 'I don't want to buy anything. I'm just trying to find my wife and the minute I start talking to a pretty girl, she'll be here.'

Short

Sir Gordon Richards was the first professional jockey to be knighted. He said, 'Mother always told me my day was coming but I never realised I'd end up being the shortest knight of the year.'

I just read that Ronnie Corbett had his pocket picked. Now that's what I call stooping low.

I try not to talk down to him but it isn't easy.

Show Biz

Comedian Fred Allen once said, 'My agent gets ten per cent of everything I get, except my blinding headaches.'

Morecambe and Wise did a charity show for a pal who sent them each a beautiful watch. To be sure their agent participated in all income they phoned him every hour and told him what time it was.

George Burns told Bob Hope it was time he retired. Hope said, 'I'm 15 years younger than you. Why don't you retire?' Burns said, 'I can't, I'm booked up.'

Lord Delfont passed a building site and saw a man do five back somersaults and a head spin. He said, 'I'll book you for the Palladium.' The man said, 'You'll have to book Paddy as well. He's the one burned my bum with his blow-torch.'

Signs

I saw it on our office noticeboard: 'For sale, 1979 sports car, as new, price absurdly high, owner loves to haggle.'

At our library entrance is a notice: 'Welcome, Silent Majority.'

On our computer room door it says, 'Authorised Personnel Only. If You Have to Ask, You Aren't.'

I rather liked the sign on the Rank Xerox van: 'Please drive carefully, We can't duplicate *you*.'

At my local garage a sign says, 'We require a 50 per cent deposit from customers we don't know. And a 100 per cent deposit from some we do know.'

In my local estate agents: 'Buy Land – It's Not Being Made Any More.'

In an antique shop: 'There's No Present Like The Past.'

In a jeweller's: Give her something to wrap around her little finger besides you.'

On my accountant's wall: 'There's no such thing as petty cash.'

We have a local spiritualist who has a sign on her door: 'Please ring bell. Knocking causes confusion.'

In a furniture shop: 'The best beds for love or money.'

In a Dublin pub: 'Never Drink on an Empty Pocket.'

Silence

There's nothing wrong with having nothing to say as long as you don't insist on saying it.

You can tell when (name) has nothing to say. His lips move.

It's easier to suffer along in silence if you're *positive* someone is watching.

To save face, keep lower half shut.
Silence is not only golden ... it's seldom misquoted.

Sincerity

Remember the words of Hughie Green. 'Always be sincere ... even if you don't mean it.'

Smiles

I like to see a broad smile especially if she smiles at me.
If you want to drive your wife crazy, don't talk in your sleep, just smile.

Speeches

I love a finished speaker.
I really, truly do.
I don't mean one who's polished,
I just mean one who's through.
(Name) was in the middle of a speech when someone at the rear shouted, 'I can't hear you!' – and a man at the front yelled back, 'I'll change places with you!'
Speeches are like babies – easy to conceive but hard to deliver.

Success

The height of success in this world is having one's name written everywhere ... except in the telephone directory.
He's a success thanks to a combination of luck and pluck ... the luck of finding people to pluck.
I know an immigrant who came to this country only ten years ago and already that man owes £980,000.
The recipe for success is the same as for a nervous breakdown!
Be nice to people on the way up – because you might get stuck between floors and want to kill a little time.

Survival

Granddad had a long and hard life. I once asked him how he'd made it through two World Wars, the Depression, and a lot of other trials. He said, 'The Bible, my boy. Time and again it says, "And it came to pass". But never once will you find it saying, "And it came to stay".'

Tax

This Tax Inspector saw a psychiatrist. He said, 'I get the feeling that the whole world hates me.' The doctor said, 'What nonsense, the whole world doesn't

hate you. The people of this country, yes, but not the whole world.'
I always put a dab of perfume on my tax return. Considering what they're doing to me, I might as well get them in the mood.
I said to my Tax Inspector, 'Have a heart!' He took it.

Teens

Teenagers are also parent agers.
My son and I have a Siamese Twin relationship. We're joined at the wallet.
He yelled at me, 'I didn't ask to be born!' I yelled back, 'Good thing you didn't – I'd have turned you down.'

Television

Most of man's inventions have been time-savers … then came television.
As Terry Wogan has said, 'The trouble with being a TV star is that you wind up in everyone's home but your own.'
I once overheard a TV director saying to an actress, 'More sincerity! This isn't just a line from some play, it's the commercial!'
I worry about all the time my children spend watching TV. My six-year-old only seems to know one word – 'Sshhh!'
Invited to watch television, a very old lady up from the country said, 'No thanks, I've already seen it.'

Time

There's an old Irish proverb: God made time, but man made haste.
The banker's analysis of time: yesterday is a cancelled cheque, tomorrow is a promissory note, but today is cash – spend it wisely.
Austin Dobson said it: 'Time goes, you say? Ah no! Alas, time stays, we go.'
Will Rogers said, 'Half our life is spent trying to find something to do with the time we've rushed through life trying to save.'
By the time you find greener pastures, you're too old to climb the fence.

Towns

When you return to your boyhood town, you find it wasn't the town you longed for. It was your boyhood.

Travel

I asked my travel agent when is the best time to go to Tahiti and he said, 'Any time between 21 and 45.'
I overheard two ladies: 'Just came back from Mykonos.' 'Where's Mykonos?' 'I don't know, we flew.'

Driving down to Leatherhead, we got lost in the Surrey countryside and called out to a farmhand, 'Leatherhead?' To which he shouted back, 'Pigface!'

I get home so seldom that when I'm seen around the house, the neighbours gossip.

Troubles

Personally I always tell my troubles to my enemies. They are the only ones who really want to hear them.

Look out of the window from the breakfast table and you see the bird after the worm, the cat after the bird, and the dog after the cat. It gives you a little better understanding of the morning's news.

Truth

Remember Diogenes with his lamp searching for an honest man? Today he'd have to settle for a dishonest man who felt guilty about it.

The Greatest Lie of the 20th century: My vasectomy left no scar.

They say George Washington could never tell a lie. My wife can. As soon as she hears it.

Truth is hard to find. That's why I hardly believe anything I hear and only half of what I say. (Not that I ever lie, I just tell the truth creatively.)

Unemployment

When it comes to solving unemployment the Government just won't take *now* for an answer.

The Government's concerned with a working majority. They should do more to get a majority working.

There's one nice thing about not having a job. When you get up in the morning, you're already there.

Universities

Freddie 'Parrot Face' Davies said of student unrest: 'I liked it the way it used to be, when student bodies were only interested in other student bodies.'

Value

Never tell a woman you're unworthy of her love. She knows.

How much would you be worth if you lost all your money?

War

Herodotus said it: 'In peace, sons bury their fathers. In war, fathers bury their sons.' World War Three is unique because it will never be mentioned in the history books.

Waste

Nothing is more wasted than a smile on the face of a slender girl with a 40-inch bust.

Weather

There's one good thing about snow ... it makes my garden look just as nice as my neighbour's.

My doctor advised me to walk more and I've learned something – bad weather always looks much worse through a window.

My grandfather used to say no matter how bad the weather is, it's better than none at all. I never did understand that man.

Wedding Anniversary

To ensure the success of our dinner party, I made all the arrangements including an iced layer cake with the inscription 'YOU ARE MY ONE AND ONLY' and I asked the caterers to make it a great big 'ONE'. When the cake was brought in I had the delicate task of explaining to my wife, who is sensitive about her weight, why the inscription read. 'TO MY GREAT BIG ONE AND ONLY'.

My wife gave me something I always wanted ... she let me win in an argument.

A Crystal Anniversary: 15 years of my wife being able to see right through me.

A Paper Anniversary: 10 years of coming home to find a note saying my dinner's in the oven.

Winning

A great philosopher once said, 'Nice guys finish last.' Or was it a great nymphomaniac?

Wives

The ideal wife is one who remains faithful to you but tries to be just as agreeable as if she weren't.

The wife who insists on wearing the trousers usually finds some other woman is wearing the mink.

When your wife asks to see something more expensive, she's shopping. When she asks to see something cheaper, she's buying.

Wives are smarter ... they never marry a man for his big boobs.

Work

The 40-hour week has no charm for me. I'm looking for the 40-hour day.

Quite a few people are already working a 4-day week. Trouble is it takes them five or six days to do it.

If you've got to work for an idiot, you might as well work for yourself.
Pitch in and do your part. Some day we won't have a part to pitch in.

World, The

One problem with the world is that so many people who stand up vigorously for their rights fall down miserably on their duties.
If we want to make a new world we certainly have the material ready ... first one was made out of chaos.
My eight-year-old was writing busily and she told me, 'I'm writing an essay on the world.' 'That's a pretty tall order.' 'Not really, three of us in my class are working on it.'
The world is full of willing people. Half willing to work, the rest willing to let them.

Yawns

If you happen to yawn while I'm speaking, I won't mind. A yawn is Nature's way of letting married men open their mouths.
I can't stop yawning. They put me on a course of iron tablets and I came down with metal fatigue.

Youth

Youth calls to youth, which is as it should be ... but it probably explains why the rest of us can't get to the phone.

Special occasions

JEWISH GATHERINGS

'In our religion,' explained the jolliest of our great Jewish actors Alfred Marks in a speech, 'the sin of eating bread on Passover is comparable to committing adultery. I told this to your Chairman and he tells me he's tried them both and can't see the comparison.'

Alfred's advice to me was a little more practical: 'To an audience that's one hundred per cent Jewish, you can get away with almost any good Yiddisher story. But with a large percentage of non-Jewish people present, even the best of those jokes can sound racist. So play it safe. Only use a tale that pokes affectionate or respectful fun at God's Chosen.' And he gave me these lovely examples:

They named a Jewish holiday after my sex life ... Passover.

My neighbour is half-Jewish and half-Irish. He drinks unleavened Guinness. My other neighbour is half-Jewish and half-Mormon. His family came from Salt Beef City.

The Rabbi told all the children to say their prayers at night ... because you can send cheap-rate messages after six o'clock.

This Israeli soldier apologised for capturing only eight tanks and 250 prisoners. The soldier's exact explanation was: 'After all, my husband wasn't with me.'

Ginsberg the tailor was dying and he told his brother the solicitor, 'Take this down. To my four daughters I leave £100,000 each. To my only son, I leave £250,000. To each of my grandchildren, £50,000 ....' His brother says, 'Wait! What are you talking about? Your entire estate isn't worth more than a couple of thousand pounds. Where are they going to get the money?' And Ginsberg said, 'Let them go out and work for it like I did!'

Last summer in Bournemouth it was so hot the women weren't even wearing their mink coats on the beach. Just the insurance valuations.

Two little boys are talking: 'Hey, Manny, what's nine and five?' Manny says, 'Are you buying or selling?'

If there is a very well-known and well-regarded person in the room who is widely recognised as a prominent Jewish member of the audience, this tale registers nicely:

Earlier this evening a few of us got into a slight argument about which were more intelligent, horses or pigs. I said pigs were smarter, they understood more words and you never see a pig run into a burning barn like some horses do. (Someone else) said I was wrong – horses like Trigger and Silver and other famous Hollywood names all displayed great learning ability. And then they got put out to stud which was the cleverest move of all. Then (Jewish personality) came up and said, 'What's the argument?' We said, 'You can settle it for us. Which are smarter – pigs or horses?' And he said, 'Jews are smarter than either. We don't bet on horses and we don't eat pigs.'

He plays orthodox golf. Never drives on Saturday.

Here's a scene on a plane flying to Rome. In one seat, a little Jewish tailor on his way to Israel. Sitting next to him, a big angry-looking Arab. The Arab dozes off but the tailor feels airsick. And he is. All over the Arab. The Arab wakes up. And there's the little tailor, patting him and saying, 'There, there – feeling better now?'

When a poor man eats chicken, one of them is ill.

Goldblum is knocked down by a car. A passerby puts his coat under Goldblum's head and asks, 'Are you comfortable?' Goldblum says, 'Listen, I make a living.'

Little Morrie Mendel asks his father, 'Pop, what's business ethics?' Mendel Senior says, 'I'll give you an example, my son. A customer comes into the shop, buys a shirt and pays for it with a £20 note. As he's walking out the door I realise that he's given me two £20 notes stuck together. Now here's where the question of business ethics comes in. Should I or should I not tell my partner?' What's a Jewish grandmother's favourite nine-letter word? 'Eateateat!'

Goldbloom tells Schwartz he's got a £250,000 order from Marks and Spencer. Schwarz says, 'I don't believe it.' Goldbloom says, 'You don't believe it? Here, I'll show you the cancellation!'

I said to my tailor, 'Mr. Cohen, you promised to make me that suit in two weeks and a whole month has gone by.' He said, 'It's almost finished.' I said, 'Almost? Mr. Cohen, it only took six days for the Lord to make the world.' He said, 'First, I want you should examine the suit, such workmanship, such cloth, such style! Now go to the window and take a look at that shitty world.'
The tailoring business was in trouble. Cohen said, 'If only the Messiah would come!' Levy said, 'How would that help us? 'Cohen said, 'He would raise the dead and they'd all need new clothes.' Levy said, 'Ahah, but that would bring back all the dead tailors and we'd have too much competition.' And Cohen said, 'Idiot, they wouldn't know the styles!'

Goldfarb's walking down a dark alley when he's stopped by a thief with a gun: 'Hand over the money!' Goldfarb pulls out the whole day's takings, £200. He peels off one £10 note and hands over the rest. The thief says, 'What's your game?' Goldfarb says, 'It's a cash transaction. You're going to refuse me five per cent discount?'

Mrs. Levy meets Mrs. Moskowitz: 'What have you done to your hair? It looks like a wig!' 'It *is* a wig.' 'It is? My God, you'd never know it!'
Then there was this one-fingered Jewish pickpocket. He specialised in stealing bagels.

I know a dentist with such a huge respect for religion, he treated a vicar and refused the fee. And that vicar was so grateful, he sent the dentist a Bible as a gift. Another time, a Catholic priest came to him for treatment, again he refused payment and the priest sent him a silver crucifix. Soon after that, a rabbi came in for dental work, the dentist refused payment and the rabbi sent him another rabbi.

LINES FOR A WEDDING SPEECH

Straight away I want to refute the vicious rumour that's been going around here today that the bride and groom *had* to get married. That's a wicked lie. They could easily have waited another fortnight.

Although I do hope the bride is expecting a little one. Otherwise she's going to be disappointed tonight.
(*NB: Don't use either of those lines unless you're certain that the crowd is broadminded and the bride isn't pregnant.*)

I've already congratulated the groom, I said, 'Old pal, you will always look back on this day as the happiest of your life.' This was yesterday.

This marriage will last a lifetime and that's unusual these days. I know a couple who broke up before their wedding pictures were developed. And they were Polaroid.

Traditionally June is supposed to be the month for weddings. This year alone, if all the June honeymoon couples in Britain were put end to end, they'd be doing it all wrong.

It was a beautiful ceremony. I found it very moving to see my old pal taking his two marriage vows – Silence and Poverty.

But our lovely bride has always said she wanted a very simple wedding and that's what she got – starting with the groom.

There are some wonderful wedding presents – toasters and saucepans – I hope he likes boiled toast.

I sent my wedding present last week and I've already received a charming thank-you note from the bride to say it was just what she wanted and she'd use them every time she entertained friends. Now I'm worried. I gave her bedsheets.

I gave the groom a book called *The Joy of Sex*. I thought he could take it on the honeymoon and read it during his off moments.

I've been worried for the groom ever since that moment at the altar. The rest of you weren't close enough to hear this – but when the vicar said, 'You may kiss the bride,' she said, 'Not now, I've got a headache.'

What advice can I give our newlyweds from my vast store of experience and wisdom? Well, for one thing, be sure to keep your Marriage Licence in a very safe place because it's one of the most important documents you will ever have. You can't get a divorce without it.

Advice to the groom? Easy. When she hands you a dishcloth, blow your nose on it and hand it back.

To the father of the bride I can only say this. You're not losing a daughter, you're gaining a bathroom.

In the words of the song, you've 'only just begun'. There are bound to be a few little mistakes in a new marriage. Remember the newly-wed couple who didn't know the different between putty and vaseline? A week later all their windows fell out. Which was the least of their worries.

None of the married men here will forget their wedding nights. Pyjamas under the pillow in case there's a fire. And your bride coming shyly from the bathroom, all coy and cute in her new nightie, he hair falling softly around her perfumed shoulders, a vision of feminine beauty and desire. Next morning she's up early before you wake up to put on her make-up for breakfast ....

Give it six months. She flops into bed in Hilda Ogden curlers, half a pound of Trex on her puss, dressed for an army assault course. She comes to the breakfast table looking as if she came second in a suicide contest. And if the doorbell rings she says, 'You go. I can't let the milkman see me like this!'

It's important to establish the ground rules early in a marriage. My dad did that. Just as soon as they'd arrived in the bridal suite, he took his trousers off, tossed them to his bride and said, 'Put 'em on!' My mum gave him a funny look but she put them on and said, 'Well?' He said, 'That, my dear, is the first and last time you wear the trousers in this marriage.' She took his trousers off, pulled off her knickers and threw them at him. She said, 'Put *them* on! He said, 'I'll never get into *them*!' She said, 'No, and until you change your attitude, sweetheart, you won't!'

(*Mike Reid told me that final story and it's a very popular gag. Mike tells it as happening to him on his own honeymoon and you may prefer to do the same.*)

LAUGHING ON RELIGIOUS GROUNDS

Every comedian has a few gags about religion in his repertoire and most churchmen have even more. I've yet to attend a function with a member of the clergy present where a good-natured joke about his calling didn't win a warm wave of laughter. You may be called upon to 'say a few words' at just such an occasion, a christening party perhaps, or a church fund-raising effort. Here are four favourites of other comedians, and a collection of my own.

Les Dawson tells the one about his vicar leaving their parish after thirty years. 'My wife said, "I'm sorry to see you go, vicar, because before you came to this neighbourhood we didn't know what sin was".'

Woody Allen declared, 'There is no God. And furthermore, try getting a plumber on a weekend.'

Ronnie Corbett knows a man of mixed parentage and religious loyalties, being part Muslim, part Hebrew and part Catholic. Three times a day he kneels towards Mecca and sings, 'Oy Vay Maria'.

Jerry Stevens says, 'Us Italian Catholics nearly had an Irish Pope, but the Vatican changed the decision at the last minute. They found out the first thing he was going to do was wallpaper the Sistine Chapel.'

Before coming here today I popped into the church, dropped £10 in the poor box and asked the vicar to bless my speech. He read it, gave me back the £10 and dropped my speech in the poor box.

I saw a minister wearing a T-shirt that said 'CLERGYMEN DO IT WITH FAITH'. That wouldn't have been so bad, but beside him was a girl wearing one that said, 'I'M FAITH.'

There's nothing like being honest with yourself and with your God. It's not always so easy being completely truthful to your minister. A woman moved into a new house near us and the vicar called. He said, 'Are you a churchgoer?' She said, 'Every Sunday to every service, vicar, until my legs wouldn't allow it. Now I just have to worship in my own way at home.' He said, 'I see, you study the Good Book?' She said, 'Constantly, vicar, all day and every day.' Then she called to her little girl, 'Tracey, go and fetch that big thick book that mummy's always reading.' And the kid came back with Kay's catalogue.

Two nuns took a stroll through the woods at twilight, two men leapt out of the bushes, ripped off the nuns' habits and had their wicked way with them. Sister Maria, shaken and shocked, looked up to heaven and cried, 'Forgive them, Lord, they know not what they do.' And Sister Kathleen looked over and said, 'Mine does.'

When you pause to think about what God created – the heavens, the earth, the mountains and valleys, the birds of the air and the beasts of the forest, and it only took Him six days. Fantastic! Only six days. It took the Council six months to put a toilet in my mother's bathroom. And that's not all – after God made the earth, he flooded it. And the same thing happened to my mother's bathroom.

Our old bishop used to say that church members are either pillars or caterpillars. The pillars hold up the church, the caterpillars just crawl in and out.

I've devoted my life to relieving morally handicapped women.

Every speaker learns to weigh carefully the meaning of each word he uses. Unlike the Muslim immigrant who went to watch a Rugby match in Wales. Before the match the Bishop of Cardiff led the teams and the crowd of 20,000 people in Christian prayer. This Muslim was so deeply moved he stood up and said, 'I want to be converted' – so they took him on the field and kicked him over the bar.

Our vicar said, 'Any person in this church was has committed adultery without shame, let him stand up.' So I stood up. He said, 'Are you without shame?' I said 'No, but I didn't like to see you standing up by yourself.'

God doesn't pay his workers large salaries – but the retirement benefits are out of this world.

My wife is a good Catholic. In fact she's such a good Catholic we can't get fire insurance – too many candles in the house.

The new vicar said to his verger, 'I think I shall devote my first sermon in this parish to "The Widow's Mite". And the Verger said, 'I shouldn't, sir. There are only two in the village and they both do.'

There's always been a degree of prejudice in every religion. The Rev. Ian Paisley saw this little Asian lad walking into his church so he whispered, 'Hey you! This is a white Protestant church, not some heathen pagan temple of six-armed demons! Go away and pray to Almighty God in Heaven for guidance!' Next day the little Asian lad came back. He said, 'Mister, I prayed to Almighty God just like you said and while I was on my knees, the Lord spoke to me.' Mr. Paisley said, 'And just what would the Almighty have to say to someone like you?' The Asian boy said, 'Sir, the Lord is saying to me, "Gupta, what are you praying for down there?" And I am saying, "Lord, I am wishing to go into Mr. Paisley's church." And the Lord, he is laughing and laughing and saying, "Sonny, you have no chance – I've been trying to get in there for twenty years myself."'

I've only attended one ecumenical conference and some of the debates spilled over into the dining areas. At one table an earnest young Catholic priest and an equally emphatic Church of England minister were arguing fiercely about whose religion was the true one. A wise old rabbi listened a while, then said, 'You are both very sincere men of the cloth, but after all, we're all working for God. All I can suggest to you is this – you two go on teaching His laws in *your* ways and I'll go on teaching His laws in *His*.'

Not being a Catholic, the only two words I know in Latin are 'Rhythm and Blues.' You use the rhythm method and when it doesn't work, you get the blues.

It's easy enough for me to stand here handing out advice. The test of it is whether or not I'd take it myself. Remember the classic story of the carpenter working in a church when he hits his thumb an almighty thump and yells, '*Bloody Hell!*' The priest hears him, rushes over and says, 'Paddy, when you hurt yourself, don't curse like that. Swearing is the very sound of evil itself. If you're in pain, instead of blasphemy and profanity just say, "Help me, Lord" and the Lord will help you.' Paddy says, 'But I split me thumb and it's bleeding and I think I broke it, father – *bloody hell!*' The priest says, 'Stop that now! What have I just been telling you?' Paddy says, 'Yes father, all right, I'll do like you say – *Help me Lord!*' A shaft of light beams down from heaven, an angel choir sings, Paddy's thumb stops bleeding, the bone knits, the skin heals up – and the priest says, '*Bloody hell!*'

Religious faith has a lot to do with your perspective. One goldfish said to the other goldfish, 'Do you believe in God?' And the other goldfish said, 'Of course I do, who do you think changes the water?'

It's amazing how easy it is to say the wrong thing in public unintentionally. Our church treasurer, Mr. Greenhill, ran off with all the funds. Our vicar stood up in the pulpit and said, 'I am very sorry to have to tell you that our church treasurer, Mr. Greenhill, has absconded with all the funds. We shall now sing hymn number 406, "There is a green hill far away."'

In the United States they have faith healers on the radio. There's an elderly couple sitting listening to the Reverend Jimmy Swaggart asking for donations and he's saying, 'All you people out there in radioland, with the Lord's help I want to heal you! Put one hand on the radio and your other hand on the part that needs healing and have faith!' The old lady puts one hand on the radio and the other on her heart. The old man puts one hand on the radio and the other in his lap. And the old lady says, 'No, George, the preacher said heal the sick, not raise the dead.'

Some of you may remember a famous bandleader of the dance band days named Roy Fox. Roy had a brother back in the USA who was a Roman Catholic priest and Roy loved to tell the story of how his brother was not wearing his priest's collar when a cop stopped him for speeding. The priest said, 'I'm Father Fox.' And the cop said, 'I don't care if you're Mother Goose, you're still getting a ticket.'

THE FINAL WORD

No matter how well you think you're doing, there's always the possibility that the man at the top will see it another way. Take the classic tale of Sergio who drops his toast and it falls on the floor with the butter and jam side *upwards!* He rushes to the priest, tells him what happened and says, 'Father, would the Church confirm that I've been blessed with an Official Miracle?' The priest thinks to himself, 'Well, Sergio always puts all his change in the collection box, I'll check it out,' so he goes to the Cardinal. The Cardinal goes to the Pope and says, 'Your Holiness, one of our devoted brethren has a member of his flock who dropped his toast and it fell on the floor with butter and jam side upwards. He wants to know – is it a miracle? What shall we tell him?' And the Pope said, 'Tell him he buttered the wrong side.'

The final word is really yours, of course, because this book is no more than a motorist's manual. How you drive is up to you. As promised, the last few pages are bare, awaiting the wise, witty and most worthwhile gleanings from other speakers, radio, TV – plus your own creative power. And if I just happen to be in the hall next time you speak, tip me the wink. I promise to laugh the loudest in all the right places. I wish you the best of luck and in Oscar Hammerstein II's famous song title, 'Happy Talk'!